Great Stories in American History

GREAT STORIES

IN

AMERICAN

HISTORY

A Selection of Events from the 15th to 20th Centuries

Rebecca Price Janney

Horizon Books

3825 Hartzdale Drive, Camp Hill, PA 17011

www.cpi-horizon.com

ISBN: 0-88965-146-9

Unless otherwise indicated, Scripture taken from the
Holy Bible: King James Version.

Scripture labeled "NIV" is taken from the HOLY BIBLE:
NEW INTERNATIONAL VERSION ®
Copyright © 1973, 1978, 1984 by the
International Bible Society. Used by
permission of Zondervan Bible Publishers.

Author photo by Isaac Bensadoun

Interior art by Sandy Helzer

To my father, Joseph Perio,
who stormed the beaches at Normandy,
fought through the Ardennes
and helped liberate Buchenwald,
and all his compatriots who,
in God's strength,
helped save the world.

Contents

Illustrations

Introduction

One of my favorite things about teaching American history is getting to share with my students God's activity in our nation's past. Most of them are astounded to discover how God planted this country and nurtured it, sustained it through the difficult times, and continues to raise up people and work in events, to fulfill His overall purpose for humanity—to call us back to Himself through His Son, Jesus Christ.

Most of these are stories that you won't find in conventional history books because most contemporary historians view the march of our past horizontally rather than vertically. God, in their eyes, has little to do with the American experience. Yet one cannot honestly look back without seeing God's fingerprints everywhere: from Columbus's motivation, to John Winthrop's stirring vision of a city on a hill, to the stern grace of the Revolutionary and Civil

Wars, to the deaf Miss America who interpreted the crucifixion through dance, although she could not hear the music.

That George Whitefield and Frances Willard show up in this book probably won't surprise you, but you may be startled to find the likes of Clarence Darrow, Albert Einstein and Benjamin Franklin within these covers. None of them was a professing Christian. How could they be in a book about God's actions in U.S. history? Because throughout history God has raised up all kinds of people to achieve His purposes. Think of Cyrus the Great of whom God said:

> For the sake of Jacob my servant,
> of Israel my chosen,
> I summon you by name
> and bestow on you a title of honor,
> though you do not acknowledge me. . . .
> I will strengthen you,
> though you have not acknowledged me,
> so that from the rising of the sun
> to the place of its setting
> men may know there is none besides me.
> I am the LORD, and there is no other.
> (Isaiah 45:4-6, NIV)

Story after story from America's past attests to the remarkable ways in which God has blessed—and continues to bless—the United States, a nation conceived in His love and bearing His likeness in so many people and events. May the words of "America, the Beautiful" ever be so:

O beautiful for heroes proved
  In liberating strife,
Who more than self their country loved,
  And mercy more than life!
America! America! May God thy gold refine,
Till all success be nobleness
  And every gain divine!

Christopher Columbus

In 1492 the Genoese voyager Christopher Columbus (1451-1506) initiated the exploration of the Americas. Sailing under the Spanish flag, he claimed the Bahamas, Cuba and Hispaniola (present-day Haiti and the Dominican Republic) for that nation's sovereigns.

Few people realize, however, that Columbus answered to a Higher Authority than the Spanish crown. According to a little-known book he wrote in Spanish, Columbus ventured out into the unknown, not for spices and precious metals alone, nor for his own glory or ego, but to win the native people's hearts to Jesus Christ. He wrote:

> It was the Lord who put into my mind (I could feel His hand upon me) the fact that it would be possible to sail from here to the Indies. All who heard of my project rejected it with laughter, ridiculing me. There is no question that the inspiration was from the Holy Scriptures.[1]

Amazingly, the navigator confessed that mathematical skills and maps were not his guide for the historical journey, but the Scriptures, which he believed foretold it. Columbus was not afraid of the perilous voyage—not when he saw himself carrying it out in Jesus' name and for the sake of His kingdom.

* * *

By October 9, 1492 Columbus and his men had been sailing since August 3 without any signs of land ahead. Some of the crew, weary of the fruitless voyage and the endless expanse of unyielding ocean, threatened to mutiny if Columbus didn't turn around and head back to Spain. The commander asked for three more days. If they hadn't spotted land by then, Columbus promised to lead them home.

Two days later men on the *Pinta* and the *Niña* found floating on the water pieces of carved wood, a reed and a twig. They couldn't be too far from land! At 10 o'clock that night Columbus noticed a flicker of light being raised and lowered in the distance ahead. At 2 o'clock on the morning of the 12th the *Pinta*'s sailors cried out, "Tierra! Tierra!" (Land! Land!)

Around noon that day, Columbus became the first European to set foot on American soil, actually a white coral beach. He carried the Spanish monarchs' banner with its green cross and Ferdinand and Isabella's crowned initials against a white backdrop. Columbus instructed his men to kneel as he christened the island "San Salvador," after the Holy Savior, Jesus.

Then the Admiral of the Ocean Sea lifted his voice to the heavens:

O Lord, Almighty and everlasting God, by Thy holy Word Thou hast created the heaven, and the earth, and the sea; blessed and glorified be Thy Name, and praised be Thy Majesty, which hath deigned to use us, Thy humble servants, that Thy holy Name may be proclaimed in this second part of the earth.[2]

Pocahontas

Pocahontas (c. 1595-1617) was an Indian princess whose father, Powhatan, ruled some thirty Tidewater, Virginia tribes. When the English began to settle Jamestown in 1607, Pocahontas became a frequent visitor to the fort. Tomboyish and delightful, she won the Englishmen's hearts, often taking them gifts of food to relieve their hunger when supplies ran low.

The Indian princess also provided a buffer between her people and the British, and Powhatan may have encouraged his daughter's relationships with the colonists to secure their support in his battles with other tribes. At any rate, Pocahontas helped make the Jamestown settlement work by promoting positive relations between her people and the English.

In the spring of 1613 Captain Samuel Argall detained Pocahontas as a kind of hostage in the Jamestown fort, using her to secure the release of English prisoners from some Tidewater Indians as well as to establish a permanent peace with that tribe.

The Englishmen treated Pocahontas well, and Powhatan was not alarmed by the incident. During that period, his daughter became a Christian and took the name Rebecca at her baptism.

Her conversion seems to have been due, in part, to the efforts of the widower John Rolfe, the man who introduced tobacco to Virginia from the West Indies. He fell in love with Pocahontas and petitioned Jamestown's Governor Thomas Dale for permission to marry her. In the letter he explained that his motivation was:

> but for the good of this plantation, for the honour of our countrie, for the glory of God, for my owne salvation, and for the converting to the true knowledge of God and Jesus Christ, an unbeleeving creature, namely Pokahuntas.[1]

Powhatan considered the marriage a wise political move; the couple wed in April 1614.

Their union promoted peace between the English settlers and the Indians. It is interesting to speculate what the country might have been like if more Europeans had followed Rolfe's example. Many problems and hostilities between the races might have been avoided had there been more intermarriage during the pre-revolutionary period of American history.

Three years after Pocahontas married John Rolfe, the couple sailed with their son, Thomas, to England. There the Indian princess became a favorite in the court of King James I and Queen Anne. Among England's wealthy, the Rolfes drummed up support for colonization, motivated largely by a zeal to Christianize America.

Pocahontas was never to return to her native land, however. In March 1617 she contracted smallpox and died in England.

The most famous incident of her life happened when she was about twelve years old. No doubt smitten with the dashing Englishman Captain John Smith, Pocahontas put her own life on the line when her father threatened to take Smith's. Jared Sparks retells the story.

* * *

"Two large stones were brought in and placed before Powhatan, and Smith was dragged up to them and his head was placed upon them, that his brains might be beaten out with clubs. The fatal weapons were already raised, and the stern executioners looked for the signal, which should bid them descend upon the victim's defenseless head. But the protecting shield of divine Providence was over him, and the arm of violence was arrested. Pocahontas, the King's favorite daughter—at that time a child of twelve or thirteen years of age—finding that her piteous entreaties to save the life of Smith were unavailing, rushed forward, clasped his head in her arms, and laid her own upon it, determined either to save his life, or share his fate. Her generous and heroic conduct touched her father's iron heart, and the life of the captive was spared. . . .

"The account of this beautiful and most touching scene, familiar as it is to every one, can hardly be read with unmoistened eyes. The incident is so dramatic and startling, that it seems to preserve the freshness

of novelty amidst a thousand repetitions. We could almost as reasonably expect an angel to have come
down from heaven, and rescued the captive, as that his
deliverer should have sprung from the bosom of
Powhatan's family. The universal sympathies of mankind and the best feelings of the human heart have redeemed this scene from the obscurity which, in the
progress of time, gathers over all but the most important events. . . . Had we known nothing of her, but
what is related of her in this incident, she would deserve the eternal gratitude of the inhabitants of this
country; for the fate of the colony may be said to have
hung upon the arms of Smith's executioners."[2]

Pilgrims and Puritans

During the lengthy reign of England's Elizabeth I, the Anglican Church once again became the official religious institution. (Her older sister, Mary, had reinstated Roman Catholicism from 1553-58.) Tensions remained, however. A group of highly educated people struggled with the similarities that the Anglican Church still bore to its Roman counterpart. Known as the Puritans because they wanted to purify Anglicanism, they objected to the elaborate liturgical robes that the clergy wore, as well as to the use of candles, incense, and music in worship. Instead, the Puritans emphasized Bible study that could be understandable to ordinary people. They also emphasized that faith alone, as opposed to good works, could get a person into heaven.

While most Puritans believed in reforming the Anglican Church from within, others wanted to separate from that institution. The "Separatists" or "Pilgrims" left England in 1606 for Leyden in Holland in order to practice their beliefs unencumbered by the state church. After a dozen years of finding mostly menial employment, the Pilgrims decided to seek a place where they might have full religious liberty and live above a subsistence level. Their ship, the *Mayflower*, left for America in 1620.

Back in England, the Puritans found they could live with the government and their consciences under King James I until the moral climate got progressively worse and the Church did little to mend those crooked ways. Not only were streets polluted with human waste, but inwardly people were dirty and crude, and life was cheap:

> London was an accurate spiritual barometer for the rest of the country, for England had become a nation without a soul. A beggar could die of exposure in a merchant's doorway, and the merchant, arriving to open up in the morning would be irate at having to step over the body, and would fret about how bad it might be for business until it was disposed of.[1]

Under James I's successor, Charles I and his favorite cleric, William Laud, the Puritans suffered persecution, and many went to prison. When in March, 1629 Charles dismissed the parliament,

> . . . it looked as if he had succeeded in suppressing the traditional liberties of Englishmen. It was time for the weak, the indifferent, and the faint-hearted to run to cover. But the Puritan, doubting nothing and fearing no man, under-

took to set all crooked ways straight and create a new heaven and a new earth. If he were not permitted to do that in England, he would find some other place to establish his City of God.[2]

A Pilgrim Blessing

The *Mayflower* sailed out of England in the fall of 1620 after several delays; the Puritans would arrive in their new colony at the worst possible time of year. After a tumultuous sixty-four-day journey across the Atlantic, they arrived at Cape Cod on November 9, committing themselves to a *compact* (a written agreement) that would lead away from the rule of kings and queens toward democratic self-government. In December they settled at Plymouth, constructing primitive huts in which to weather the cruel Massachusetts winter. Many fell sick, leading to the deaths of over half the 102 immigrants.

Their leader, Governor William Bradford, vividly described their grim, almost desperate, situation:

> If they looked behind them, there was the mighty ocean which they had passed and was now as a main bar and gulf to separate them from all the civil parts of the world. . . . What could now sustain them but the Spirit of God and His grace? May not and ought not the children of these fathers rightly say, "Our fathers were Englishmen which came over this great ocean, and

were ready to perish in this wilderness; but they cried unto the Lord, and He heard their voice and looked on their adversity. . . ."[3]

Considering that the group of mostly peasants, town laborers and shopkeepers were ill-suited to lives in the wilderness of a new land, they came through their ordeal remarkably well. As Bradford put it, "they knew they were pilgrims, and looked not much on those things, but lift up their eyes to the heavens, their dearest country." Another Pilgrim said, "It is not with us as with other men, whom small things can discourage, or small discontentments cause to wish themselves at home again."[4] They weathered the early storms in God's strength, to fulfill His purposes.

The Pilgrims were fortunate to make good use of some deserted fields ready for planting and were heartened by the friendship of Squanto, a native who taught them how to catch fish and plant corn. Nevertheless, half the Pilgrims did not survive that first winter. When the *Mayflower* headed back to England in April, however, not one of the survivors returned.

By the fall of 1621, the Pilgrims had reaped a fair harvest and rejoiced in a big yield of waterfowl and wild turkey. In October they held their first Thanksgiving feast, inviting Chief Massasoit of the Wampanoag tribe and ninety of his subjects, whom they entertained for three days. The Indians brought several deer as their contribution to the celebration.

That first Thanksgiving appeared to be the end of the settlers' hardship, but after thirty-five new Pilgrims arrived the colony soon found itself short on provisions, just steps away from famine. Although this state of affairs lasted for several years, the colonists refused to give up and go back to England.

These simple folk were exalted to the stature of statesmen and prophets in their narrow sphere, because they ardently believed, and so greatly dared, and firmly endured. They set forth in acts as in words the stout-hearted idealism in action that Americans admire; that is why Plymouth Rock has become a symbol. For, as Governor Bradford concluded his annals of the lean years, "Thus out of small beginnings greater things have been produced by His hand that made all things of nothing, and gives being to all things that are; and as one small candle may light a thousand; so the light here kindled hath shone unto many, yea, in some sort, to our whole nation.[5]

John Winthrop and the City on a Hill

In 1628 the Council for New England issued a grant to a group of Puritans to establish a settlement between the Charles and Merrimack Rivers. Sixty-six men under soldier John Endecott inhabited the area around present-day Salem; they were later joined by another group of 200 men. The Puritans eventually gained control of these endeavors and secured a royal charter as the "Governor and Company of the Massachusetts Bay in New England."[6]

A group of now-distinguished Cambridge University alumni gathered in late summer 1629, signing an agreement to emigrate to New England sometime within the next seven months. (Although they planned to join the colony in Salem, the royal charter had to be worded very carefully so that it did not require them to locate in a particular place. Otherwise it could have been revoked.) The group also elected a governor, a lawyer named John Winthrop.

The Puritans went to New England for a divine purpose, not for material or personal gain. They viewed New England as a New Canaan that God would use as an experiment in Christian living, "a city upon a hill" for all the world to see.[7]

In March of 1630 Winthrop departed England on the flagship *Arbella* with one son and fifteen other ships, leaving behind his vast estate, his wife and his second son.

Halfway between England and the New World, Winthrop preached a sermon, "A Modelle of Christian Charity," on the *Arbella's* deck. With an ocean breeze stirring his dark hair, Winthrop issued this challenge:

> We must Consider that wee shall be as a Citty upon a Hill, the eies of all people are upon us; soe that if wee shall deale falsely with our God in this worke wee have undertaken and soe cause him to withdrawe his present help from us, wee shall open the mouthes of enemies to speake evill of the wayes of God and all professours for Gods sake.[8]

After a peaceful voyage, which the Puritans considered a sign of God's favor upon their bold experiment, the intrepid Englishmen first set eyes on America. Winthrop was captivated by the tall pine trees, but became disturbed upon finding the Salem settlement in a dilapidated state. Of the nearly 300 men who had gone before, only 85 were left and they were ready to give up. The rest had died or returned to England in discouragement. Winthrop spent a sleepless night on the *Arbella* wondering whether the Puritans' plan was doomed to fail. Perhaps he hadn't heard God correctly. Maybe He really didn't intend the Puritans to be "a Citty upon a Hill." His fears, however, quickly vanished as God boosted his sagging spirit. Winthrop knew that with the Lord's help and his company's obedience, the experiment in Christian living would succeed. He wrote:

Thus stands the cause between God and us: we are entered into covenant with Him for this work. We have taken out a Commission; the Lord hath given us leave to draw our own articles. . . . If the Lord shall please to hear us, and bring us in peace to the place we desire, then hath he ratified this Covenant and sealed our Commission, [and] will expect a strict performance of the Article contained in it. But if we shall neglect the observance of this Article . . . the Lord will surely break out in wrath against us.

Now the only way to avoid this shipwreck and to provide for our posterity, is to follow the counsel of Micah, to do justly, to love mercy, to walk humbly with our God. For this end, we must be knit together in this work as one man. . . . We must hold a familiar commerce together in all meekness, gentleness, patience, and liberality. We must delight in each other, make one another's condition our own, rejoice together, mourn together, labor and suffer together, always having before our eyes our Commission and Community in this work, as members of the same body. So shall we keep the unity of the Spirit in the bond of peace. . . .

We shall find that the God of Israel is among us, when ten of us shall be able to resist a thousand of our enemies, when He shall make us a praise and glory, that men of succeeding plantations shall say, "The Lord make it like that of New England."[9]

William Penn's Holy Experiment

According to historian Samuel Eliot Morison, "The founding of Pennsylvania, more so than any other American commonwealth, is the lengthened shadow of one man and of his faith in God and human nature."[1] That man was William Penn.

Admiral Sir William Penn and Margaret Jasper Penn celebrated the birth of their son, William, in London on October 14, 1644. Born to privilege and rank, young William studied law and managed his father's vast properties in Ireland. He converted to the Society of Friends—the Quakers—in his twenties under the influence of Thomas Loe, a famous preacher.

The authorities sent Penn to prison twice, including a stay in the Tower of London, because his outspoken beliefs conflicted with England's religious establishment. The Church of England was determined to crush Quakerism, which insisted that all people were equal and that they should not be forced to worship in a certain prescribed way.

In spite of dismal conditions, Penn spent his imprisonments productively, writing treatises such as *The Great Cause of Liberty of Conscience* that made a case for religious tolerance. He also wrote his best-known book, *No Cross, No Crown*, while in prison.

In 1677 Penn went to America with the famous Quaker, George Fox. While there he wrote a charter for Quaker colonists in New Jersey called the "Concessions and Agreements." The charter advocated such rights as trial by jury and freedom from arbitrary imprisonment for debt, foreshadowing the Declaration of Independence which would be written a century later. It also limited the use of capital punishment to cases of treason and murder.

The charter's most innovative clause was the one which advocated religious freedom. Penn believed that no power or authority could rightly rule over a person's conscience in religious matters. Even in America the Quakers had run into problems when severe laws were passed against them. It is understandable, therefore, that Penn came to believe so fervently in the freedom to worship God in one's own way.

A decade later, in 1681, the government of King Charles II, which was more favorable to Quakers, gave Penn a 45,000-acre land grant in the New World to fulfill a debt to the elder William. This made him England's largest landholder after the King. Penn traveled to his new colony in 1682 with several friends to establish what would be called "Pennsylvania" in honor of his father. (He had suggested "New Wales" and "Sylvania," fearing that people would think Penn had named the area after himself and not his father, but the king's wish for the name Pennsylvania prevailed.) Like the Puritans before him, Penn desired to organize a godly and upright society to inspire all the world. One historian has said that "Penn planned to give his fellow zealots, under shelter of himself as proprietor, a widely tolerant refuge that would also show the world how near an unworldly society could come to God's way. The aim was akin to New England's, though less shrill and apocalyptic."[2] He prayed for God to bless his "holy experiment," to make it "the seed of a nation."[3]

Another historian recorded, "Pennsylvania was a portent of America to be; the first large community in modern history where different races and religions lived under the same government on terms of equality."[4]

Part of Penn's plan was to extend the hand of friendship to the natives of Pennsylvania, to include them in the circle of brotherhood and tolerance. Rather than seize their land forcibly and subject them, as others had done, Penn offered the Indians a treaty and payment for their land. The famous painting of Penn's signing the treaty under a broad elm tree appears in the Capitol Rotunda in Washington, D.C. Though the incident is doubted by most contemporary historians, it reflects Penn's honorable intentions and the subsequent results of his "holy experiment." The story may be seen as symbolic of the way he actually conducted his affairs with the Native Americans.

* * *

Roughly four weeks after Penn's arrival in the New World, he met a group of sachems, or Native American kings, under an elm tree at a place called

Shackamaxon where tribal meetings often took place. The chiefs were resplendent in ceremonial garb composed of deerskin leggings, squirrel-lined mantles and elaborate feather headdresses or headbands made from snakeskin. To communicate his own rank, William Penn wore his sky-blue officer's sash over his usual Quaker gray outfit. Flanking Penn were his deputy, a man history recalls simply as "Markham," Thomas Holme, a surveyor, and several settlers. The sachems' delegation included about a hundred braves and the tribes' wisest men.

Sitting in the center of a half-circle was the chief of the Unami tribe of Delawares, Taminent, who clearly was in charge of the Native Americans of that area. He went on to become one of Penn's closest friends. To him Penn spoke the word *itah*, meaning, "Good be to you." It was all the Delaware he knew. An interpreter conveyed Penn's message of good will. "We are met on the broad pathway of good faith and good will," he said, "so that . . . all will be openness, brotherhood, and love."[5]

To facilitate positive relations between the English and the Indians, Penn told Taminent that the white men's doors always would be open to the Indians and that if any disruptions occurred between them, a special committee of representatives from both groups would decide the outcome. "I consider us all the same flesh and blood, joined by one heart," he concluded.[6]

The great sachem and his counselors spoke among themselves, then Taminent got up and shook Penn's hand. As long as the sun and moon shone, he said, their people would live in a spirit of love and friendship. To seal their fellowship, Taminent gave Penn a

special belt that portrayed them at that special moment, hand-in-hand. The French writer Voltaire once
said that this was the only treaty between Indians and
whites that was never broken.[7]

The Great Awakening of a
Friendship—and a Nation

The colonization of America began with a company of dedicated Christians determined to bring the gospel of Jesus Christ to the New World. By the opening years of the eighteenth century, however, zealousness for Christian living and evangelism had waned like an old moon. Then God sent a powerful revival, a movement known as the Great Awakening, that swept like a forest fire throughout the entire eastern seaboard. "Not one colony or county was unaffected by the Great Awakening," one textbook says. "Intermittently, but over the entire decade of the 1740's, it raged through New England, the Middle Colonies, and the South."1

Through the preaching of Jonathan Edwards, John Wesley, David Brainerd, William and Gilbert Tennent, and especially George Whitefield, Americans "were beginning to discover a basic truth . . . which by 1776 would be declared self-evident: that in the eyes of their Creator, all men were of equal value."2

The following story centers around two men who became friends during that incredible era—men used by God in profoundly different ways to prepare the way for the coming of the American nation.

* * *

Although Benjamin Franklin is not remembered as a Christian man, God used his considerable array of talents to help establish the new republic. The inventor-statesman was raised a Presbyterian but left the church as a young man largely because he found the sermons so dull. One pastor challenged him to attend his services for five Sundays, hoping to effect a change. At the end of that period, however, Franklin remained unimpressed, commenting that "not a single moral principle was inculcated or enforced, their [the sermons'] aim seeming to be rather to make us Presbyterians than good citizens."[3]

Actually Franklin echoed the frustrations of many on both sides of the Atlantic, that the Christian faith as expressed in the established churches had become merely a form of religion, lacking God's power. Franklin may not have been an orthodox believer in Christ, but he regarded the Scriptures and religion as important to upholding a just and orderly society. He supported the salaries of several ministers and helped with special projects at Christ Church in Philadelphia, where he kept a family pew.

Concerned about his lack of exclusive commitment to Christ as his Savior, Franklin's parents tried to convert him. In the months before the Great Awakening blew through Philadelphia, Franklin addressed their anxiety:

> I am sorry you should have any uneasiness on my account; and if it were a thing possible for one to alter his opinions in order to please another, I know none whom I ought more willingly to oblige in that respect than yourselves. . . . I think vital religion has always suffered when orthodoxy is more regarded than virtue; and the Scriptures assure me that at the last day we shall not be examined by what we thought but what we did; and our recommendation will not be that we said "Lord! Lord!" but that we did good to our fellow-creatures. See Matt. xxv.[4]

For Franklin, religion's place was to help people know what was right and wrong so that they could do their best to improve themselves. George Whitefield, the key figure of the Great Awakening, saw the matter differently. All people, he contended, are sinners who cannot by strength of will improve themselves enough to win God's favor. That comes only through confessing one's sins and need of the Savior, Jesus Christ, who will separate the redeemed from the lost at the final judgement. Whitefield may have seemed like an unlikely friend for Benjamin Franklin, but the truth is they became close during the preacher's stay in Philadelphia. The two men had much in common: they came from humble backgrounds and became celebrated as adults; they were fairly close in age and enthusiastic about life, both deploring the deadness of colonial Christianity.

The twenty-five-year-old Whitefield arrived in Philadelphia, then the largest city in the American colonies, in the fall of 1739. A nonconformist preacher who was derisively called an "enthusiast" by some, Whitefield preached about sin and salvation, heaven and hell. He employed his powerful voice and fervent gestures to call upon people to exchange head-knowledge of Christ for knowing the Savior in their hearts. "He made violent gestures, danced about the pulpit, roared and ranted, greatly to the delight of the common people who were tired of gentlemanly, unemotional sermons from college-bred ministers," writes Samuel Eliot Morison. "His messages were simple, direct, and taught the basic doctrines of being born again or being justified by faith. But to people who had not heard this clearly explained before, it was like a lightning shock to the heart."[5]

"I am persuaded [that] the generality of preachers talk of an unknown and unfelt Christ," Whitefield explained. "The reason why congregations have been so dead is because they had dead men preaching to them. How can dead men beget living children?"[6]

Benjamin Franklin was just as curious as the next person to see and hear this new preaching style when Whitefield came to town. Franklin wrote,

> The multitudes of all sects and denominations that attended his sermons were enormous, and it was a matter of speculation to me, who was one of the number, to observe the extraordinary influence of his oratory on his hearers, and how much they admired and respected him notwithstanding his common abuse of them by assuring them that they were naturally half beasts and half devils.[7]

On one evening the main roads surrounding Market Street swelled with some 78,000 people trying to glimpse the young English preacher. The overall effect of Whitefield's messages on Philadelphians delighted Benjamin Franklin. "It was wonderful to see the change soon made in the manners of our inhabitants," he said. "From being thoughtless or indifferent about religion, it seemed as if all the world were growing religious, so that one could not walk through the town in an evening without hearing psalms sung in different families of every street."[8]

Franklin joined the captivated throngs listening to Whitefield's outdoor sermons, messages so frank and enthusiastic that several of the city's pastors refused to let the Englishman preach from their pulpits. Even if they had, the huge crowds filling the city would have burst those churches at their seams. If Franklin missed the spiritual significance of Whitefield's sermons, he deeply admired the way the fiery preacher's voice carried. "He preached one evening from the top of the courthouse steps," Franklin said, "which are in the middle of Market Street and on the west side of Second Street, which crosses it at right angles. Being among the hindmost in Market Street, I had the curiosity to learn how far he could be heard. . . ."[9]

Under the stars of a crisp fall night while Whitefield's voice reverberated through the streets of Philadelphia, Benjamin Franklin conducted his latest experiment. As he moved slowly and carefully, Franklin heard Whitefield shout, "Father Abraham, whom have you in heaven? Any Episcopalians?"

People on the street and leaning out of their home's upper stories shouted back, "No!"

One can imagine the smiles on their faces as they glanced playfully at each other.

"Any Presbyterians?"

"No!"

"Any Independents or Seceders, New Sides or Old Sides, any Methodists?" His voice rose with the mention of each group.

"No! No! No!"

"Whom have you there, then, Father Abraham?"

Whitefield answered his own question. "We don't know those names here! All who are here are *Christians*—believers in Christ, men who have overcome by the blood of the Lamb and the word of his testimony. . . . God help me, God help us all, to forget having names and to become *Christians* in deed and in truth."[10]

By this time, Franklin had made it as far as Front Street, almost to the Delaware River, but even at that distance, Whitefield's voice still rang loudly in his ears. While people repented and angels sang them into God's kingdom, Franklin's response was purely utilitarian:

> Imagining then a semicircle, of which my distance should be the radius, and that it were filled with auditors to each of whom I allowed two square feet, I computed that he might be heard by more than thirty thousand. This reconciled me to the newspaper accounts of his having preached to twenty-five thousand people in the fields.[11]

On that occasion Franklin responded like the prisoner who in his confinement learned precisely how many words there were in the Bible but didn't have the slightest idea what they meant. Of Whitefield's sermons as a whole Franklin observed:

> His delivery . . . was so improved by frequent repetitions that every accent, every emphasis, every modulation of voice was so perfectly well turned and well placed that, without being interested in the subject, one could not help being pleased with the discourse; a pleasure of much the same kind with that received from an excellent piece of music.[12]

On at least on one occasion, however, the pastor's message penetrated Franklin's hard heart. The two men had disagreed sharply over Whitefield's plans to build an orphanage in the Georgia colony. Franklin considered the project foolhardy because it would cost far more to transport the necessary men and supplies to Georgia than it would to build the orphanage in Philadelphia and bring the children there. Whitefield prevailed. Franklin recorded:

> I happened soon after [the dispute] to attend one of his sermons, in the course of which I perceived he intended to finish with a collection [for the orphanage], and I silently resolved he should get nothing from me. I had in my pocket a handful of copper money, three or four silver dollars, and five pistoles in gold. As he proceeded I began to soften, and concluded to give the coppers. Another stroke of his oratory made me ashamed of that, and determined me to give

the silver. And he finished so admirably that I emptied my pocket wholly into the collector's dish, gold and all.[13]

Franklin went even further in his support of Whitefield's ministry. He printed the Englishman's sermons at his shop on Market Street and housed the minister in the apartment above it. And when Philadelphia's pastors continued to turn the vibrant Whitefield from their churches, Franklin bought a house "expressly for the use of any preacher of any religious persuasion who might desire to say something to the people at Philadelphia."[14]

Although Whitefield prayed ardently for his friend's conversion, Franklin said in his memoirs that Whitefield "never had the satisfaction of believing that his prayers were heard."[15] Other seeds planted by Whitefield took root, however, as God used the preacher to prepare Franklin for a leadership role in the coming struggle for independence. Whitefield's discussions of his travels in the colonies, and his keen interest in Georgia in particular, helped Franklin to regard the disparate American provinces as parts of a whole and to see that "we were a people chosen by God for a specific purpose."[16]

As the years passed, Franklin and Whitefield remained friends, frequently corresponding with each other. However, the inventor-statesman never gave his life to Christ:

> Right at the end of Whitefield's life, when Franklin was famous as diplomat, inventor, philosopher and writer, he had still not been prayed into the kingdom. Brave enough to experiment with electricity he did not dare expose himself to the lightning of the Spirit.[17]

The American Revolution

Following the French and Indian War in 1763, England signed a treaty with France that gave Britain dominance in North America. It was a great victory for the British, but it also left them with major challenges. Who was going to pay for the war, which had been fought largely on credit? How would England govern western expansion and protect the colonists from hostile Indians? Those ruling the colonies from England were largely ignorant of conditions in America and regarded its inhabitants as uncouth and inferior.

As a result of these and other factors, the British began to tighten their control on the Americans after the war. In Massachusetts general search warrants were authorized, allowing inspections without evidence or special court orders. The British did not permit Americans, other than licensed traders, to settle west of the Appalachian Mountains. And in 1764 the Revenue and Sugar Acts placed tariffs on sugar, coffee, wine and many other imported products. This led

James Otis to proclaim, "Taxation without repre-
sentation is tyranny!" Also that year, the British re-
stricted the printing of paper money in the colonies.

The outraged colonists initially failed to unite on a
strategy of resistance until 1765 brought passage of
the Stamp Act in which the British imposed taxes on
many kinds of printed matter, including newspaper
and legal documents. This provided the catalyst to
unite the colonies against British controls. An inter-
colonial Stamp Act Congress passed resolutions of
protest and colonists burned the stamps and boy-
cotted British goods.

In 1766 the British Parliament repealed the Stamp
Act, but maintained that it had the right to enact any
colonial legislation it deemed proper. When new taxes
were imposed in 1767, American leaders began questioning the basis of British colonial policy.

Tensions peaked following a snowball throwing incident against British "Redcoats" guarding the Boston
Custom House on March 5, 1770. Five Americans
died when the British soldiers panicked and fired into
the crowd, an event known to history as the Boston
Massacre.

The final crisis over British control broke out in
1773 with passage of the Tea Act in which Parliament
gave the corrupt and inefficient British East India
Company a monopoly on the colonial tea trade. The
colonists saw this as a back-door approach to requiring their submission to imperial authority. On December 16, 1773 the Boston Tea Party signaled the
beginning of a transition among Americans from being locally oriented colonists to national revolutionar-
ies.

The First Continental Congress met in the fall of 1774, passing a declaration of grievances against all British actions against the colonies since 1763. A second congress established an army in 1775, and on July 4, 1776, the Americans officially broke away from British rule. King George III regarded the "rebellion" as a challenge to his personal rule and told Prime Minister Lord North, "The die is now cast. . . . The colonies must either submit or triumph."

Give Me Liberty!

Virginian Patrick Henry (1736-1799), one of America's founding fathers, also was among its greatest orators. In the years before the Revolution, Henry farmed, practiced law and distinguished himself as a frontier representative in the Virginia House of Burgesses. He challenged England's right to tax the colonies in his Virginia Resolves in May 1765 and helped form the Committees of Correspondence that organized the colonists against illegal or offensive British actions. Henry also helped create the First Continental Congress that met in 1774 in Philadelphia.

While addressing the Virginia Convention in Richmond on March 23, 1775 about the possibility of independence, Henry urged his fellow Virginians to arm themselves against Britain, giving one of the most rousing and famous speeches in American history.

* * *

It is natural for man to indulge in the illusions of hope. We are apt to shut our eyes against a painful truth, and listen to the song of that siren till she transforms us into beasts. Is this the part of wise men, engaged in a great and arduous struggle for liberty? Are we disposed to be the number of those who, having eyes, see not, and having ears, hear not, the things which so nearly concern their temporal salvation? For my part, whatever anguish of spirit it may cost, I am willing to know the whole truth; to know the worst, and to provide for it. . . .

There is no longer room for hope. If we wish to be free, we must fight! An appeal to arms and to the God of Hosts is all that is left us!

They tell me that we are weak, but shall we gather strength by irresolution? We are not weak. Three million people, armed in the holy cause of liberty and in such a country, are invincible by any force which our enemy can send against us. We shall not fight alone. God presides over the destinies of nations, and will raise up friends for us. The battle is not to the strong alone; it is to the vigilant, the active, the brave. . . .

It is vain, sir, to extenuate the matter. The gentlemen may cry, Peace, peace! but there is no peace. The war has actually begun! The next gale that sweeps from the north will bring to our ears the clash of resounding arms! Our brethren are already in the field! What stand here idle? What is it that the gentlemen wish? What would they

have? Is life so dear, or peace so sweet, as to be purchased at the price of chains and slavery? Forbid it almighty God! I know not what course others make take, but as for me, give me liberty or give me death![1]

The Declaration of Independence

Not everyone agreed that independence was the best way for the colonists to go in their struggle against Great Britain. While Virginia passed resolutions on May 15, 1776 recommending that its delegates to the Continental Congress should propose independence, Edward Rutledge of South Carolina led the opposition. Wasn't there still hope, he argued, after all that had happened, for a reconciliation between England and her colonies? The cost to America if it pursued liberation from Britain was going to be very high. Ben Franklin knew this, and he wryly commented, "We must indeed all hang together, or most assuredly we will all hang separately."[2]

A three-week delay ensued while anxious delegates returned home to measure public opinion. Would the people stand behind the Continental Congress if it declared independence? During those weeks, Thomas Jefferson, Benjamin Franklin, John Adams, Roger Sherman and Robert R. Livingston wrote a draft of a declaration of independence. During a spirited debate in the sweltering State House (now known as Independence Hall) in

Philadelphia on July 1, John Adams, a man who had left behind his devoted wife and family, as well as his livelihood, because he believed so strongly in the cause of freedom, rose.

And he spoke with such quiet power and conviction that not a man present remained unmoved, especially as he reached his conclusion:

"Before God, I believe the hour has come. My judgement approves this measure, and my whole heart is in it. All that I have, and all that I am, and all that I hope in this life, I am now ready here to stake upon it. And I leave off as I began, that live or die, survive or perish, I am for the Declaration. It is my living sentiment, and by the blessing of God it shall be my dying sentiment, Independence now, and Independence forever!"[3]

As he concluded, Adams saw the New Jersey delegation's chairman, Dr. John Witherspoon, come through the door, wind-blown and mud-covered from his journey, announcing that New Jersey was ready to support the Declaration. "In our judgement," he declared, "the country is not only ripe for independence, but we are in danger of becoming rotten for the want of it, if we delay any longer."[4]

Nevertheless, when the delegates cast their votes, they did not reach a unanimous decision; nine said "yes," two "no." New York abstained, and Delaware split its decision. In the morning of the next day, a new vote would be taken.

Delaware's third delegate, Caesar Rodney, was summoned at his farm in Dover where a family emergency had taken him away from the proceedings. He set out after two o'clock in the morning, riding his horse eighty-nine miles through swollen streams and mucky roads created by a terrible summer storm. He exchanged his exhausted horse for a fresh one at dawn and made it to the State House in Philadelphia by one o'clock. The final vote was underway as he was led on wobbly feet into the assembly room. Utterly spent, he said barely above a whisper, "As I believe the voice of my constituents and of all sensible and honest men is in favor of independence, my own judgement concurs with them. I vote for independence."[5]

The vote ended with a 12-1 decision in favor of independence, with New York still abstaining. A hush fell over the sweltering delegates as the sun streamed through the tall, clear windows, anointing them with its light. A new nation had just come into being, a nation whose foundations were a city upon a hill for all the world to see, in the place where William Penn had begun his holy experiment a century before. John Hancock finally spoke, bringing a smile to the lips of his fellow countrymen as he declared, "Gentleman, the price on my head has just been doubled!"

Then Samuel Adams stood. "We have this day restored the Sovereign, to Whom alone men ought to be obedient. He reigns in heaven and . . . from the rising to the setting sun, may His Kingdom come."[6]

The Battle of Brooklyn Heights

J uly 4, 1776, at Philadelphia, Pennsylvania: A new nation is born to patriots longing for freedom from Great Britain and seeking to launch the most ambitious political experiment in the world's long, tired history—rule of the people, by the people and for the people.

A noble birth. But would the United States die in its infancy? Would the British Empire, the most powerful nation on earth, send the fledgling from its cradle to its grave in a matter of weeks?

How could it be otherwise? The mighty British outgunned, out-manned and out-supplied the Americans. The United States' sorry militia faced the world's most powerful army in late August, 1776 in New York. Were it not for the hand of Providence, the Battle of Brooklyn Heights would have been the last gasp of a newborn nation.

The responsibility for keeping America alive lay largely on General George Washington's shoulders as he played a cat-and-mouse game in New York throughout that sweltering summer of 1776. The Virginian had arrived in Manhattan on April 13, convinced that his British counterpart, Sir William Howe, would strike there next. Washington knew how crucial the first battle of the new country would be, that even if he didn't make major mistakes, the odds were heavily against the Americans, and if he did make mistakes, the United States of America would be remembered as the brief dream of a band of foolish rebels.

A bleaker situation is difficult to imagine. In an awesome display of strength, the British assembled the largest expeditionary force of the eighteenth century. Over 30,000 strong, it contrasted sharply with Washington's 18,000 volunteers, who were suffering from want, fear and illness. It was David vs. Goliath, the high school varsity vs. the Chicago Bulls.

In addition, American allegiance to the Declaration of Independence had yet to be tested. Was their loyalty to freedom's cause strong enough to withstand the death and destruction that British artillery surely would bring? Might it not be better to surrender while families, farms and villages remained intact? Wouldn't life under a tyrant be better than no life at all? Hadn't King George's representatives promised clemency for all those patriots who had lifted their guns and pens against him? What price liberty?

Fortunately for the beleaguered Americans, the British General Sir William Howe held no great hatred toward them. He stood among those ranks of Englishmen who regarded the patriots as naughty children who needed not an iron fist but a firm hand to bring them back into line. Upon arriving in New York, Howe waited over a month before engaging the American forces in battle. He hoped that the British show of force alone would be enough to turn the rebellious colonists into men and women who would once again bow before the throne of Britain. He didn't realize that the Americans were destined to bow before a different Throne.

On August 21 Howe finally advanced.

From his position on Manhattan, Washington sent his top 3,500 men along a forested, hilly stretch of the

East River. Another 4,000 less experienced soldiers occupied the Brooklyn Heights fort under the command of volatile Major General John Sullivan. On the morning of the 27th Howe began his campaign against Sullivan's men. Once General Washington realized that Howe was not going to attack Manhattan, he sent reinforcements across the East River to buoy Sullivan's forces that were getting squeezed by the powerful British army.

The Redcoats positioned themselves between the Brooklyn Heights fort and those American soldiers guarding it from a bluff. With a roar of gunfire a unit of German Hessians, mercenaries in Britain's employ, charged Sullivan's front.[7]

Would his men stand their ground or turn tail? Only one regiment, from Maryland, answered the call—and were almost completely wiped out, many pinned to trees by cruel British bayonets. Some 1,500 men perished. A trembling General Washington, watching the slaughter through a field telescope, cried out, "Good God, what brave fellows I must this day lose!"[8]

The survivors either ran back to the fort or surrendered to the British. Now it was up to Washington to keep the 4,000 soldiers inside the fort from panicking as massive British forces advanced toward them. One can only imagine what went through the Americans' minds. With the Brooklyn Heights fort at his mercy, General Howe delayed. Although his men outnumbered the patriots, the Americans had dug formidable earthworks. If the British stormed them, they would suffer heavy losses. No, it would be better, Howe reasoned, to employ heavy artillery against those earthworks to maximize the damage to the Americans while minimizing his own casualties. If Washington tried to escape before then, Howe would trap the American army by land and by water.

Even the best-laid plans, however, often go awry.

A praying man and a wise man, General Washington informed his officers that he was going to remove the American army from Brooklyn to Manhattan. They may have gaped as Washington explained that the evacuation would involve a flotilla of small boats ferrying group after group of soldiers for the two-mile round trip. The small craft, manned by capable Massachusetts fighters who had grown up near the water and had early learned expert oarsmanship, nevertheless would be up against the world's greatest navy.

All that storm-tossed night of the 28th the men from Massachusetts evacuated the American troops in choppy, windy conditions. When the wind dissipated around midnight, however, the moon illuminated the scene. Although more men could now flee per boat because of the calm conditions, the British would now be able to hear and see the troop movements. Also working against the Americans was their troops' fractious mood, with soldiers arguing noisily amongst themselves as they waited along the shore for their rescue. However, even under those circumstances, the British remained ignorant of Washington's evacuation.

As dawn broke, Washington knew he needed at least three more hours of darkness to complete the removal. Only a miracle could save his men—and the newborn United States.

American Major Ben Tallmadge, an eyewitness at the scene, described what happened next:

As the dawn of the next day approached, those of us who remained in the trenches became very anxious for our own safety, and when the dawn appeared there were several regiments still on duty. At this time a very dense fog began to rise [out of the ground and off the river], and it seemed to settle in a peculiar manner over both encampments. I recollect this peculiar providential occurrence perfectly well, and so very dense was the atmosphere that I could scarcely discern a man at six yards distance. . . . We tarried until the sun had risen, but the fog remained as dense as ever.[9]

When General Washington finally took the last boat to freedom, the fog began to lift. The stunned British realized what had happened: 8,000 Americans had fled under their very noses, and it was too late to do anything about it. Someday Howe and Washington would face each other again. But not that day. The hand of Providence had guided the infant nation to safety.

Valley Forge: Freedom's Crucible

In spite of an American victory at Saratoga on October 17, 1777, the Continental Army was in poor shape. Defeated at the Battle of Brandywine in September, the Americans watched helplessly as General Howe captured their capital, Philadelphia. In a vain attempt to regain the city at the Battle of Germantown on October 4, Washington's army was beaten.

The forty-six-year-old general began searching for an appropriate winter encampment for his 11,000 troops, a place beyond the reach of a surprise British attack, but where he could keep an eye on the Redcoats at the same time. He chose Valley Forge, about fifteen miles north of Philadelphia at the junction of the Schuylkill River and Valley Creek. There the American forces faced their greatest challenge.

*   *   *

Washington's exhausted troops arrived at Valley Forge on December 19, 1777, in bitter cold and snow that signaled what appeared to be the beginning of a brutal winter. On December 23 the commander-in-chief wrote to President of Congress Henry Laurens, "I am now convinced beyond a doubt that unless some great and capital change suddenly takes place in that line, this Army must inevitably be reduced to one or other of these three things. Starve, dissolve or disperse."[10]

The general immediately ordered the men to begin constructing small cabins for themselves. Building the windowless log huts gave the soldiers a way to fend off boredom as well as the cold. Squads of a dozen men worked on each cabin, vying for General Washington's prize of twelve dollars to the teams building the first properly constructed huts. Washington paid the initial reward on December 21.

The work generally went slowly, though. The men had inadequate tools with which to work, and trees had to be cut down and honed for the shelters.

Disease and lack of clothing made one out of every four men unfit for duty. Many soldiers wrapped pieces of blankets around their feet in a futile attempt at protection and warmth. The blood of their feet stained the snow at Valley Forge. After some men began cutting apart their tents to use for clothing material, Washington banned the practice; the tents would be needed the following summer. Punishment awaited any violators.

As the building of crude huts continued for several weeks, General Washington spent the nights sleeping in his own leaky tent so he could be closer to the men—not the healthiest of environments, to be sure. Under those conditions he could fall victim to pneumonia or one of the diseases spreading through the encampment.

Washington's self-sacrificial behavior, however, served to galvanize the troops' morale. Army surgeon Dr. James Thatcher noted, "The army . . . was not without consolation, for his excellency the commander-in-chief . . . manifested a fatherly concern and fellow-feeling for their sufferings and made every exertion in his power to remedy the evil and to administer the much-desired relief."[11]

But Washington's officers were not pleased; what might happen to their cause if their leader became sick, or died? In January the general finally agreed to make his headquarters in a quaint, two-story, stone house belonging to mill owner and Quaker Isaac Potts and his wife. Martha Washington rode north from Virginia to spend that trying winter with her husband to tend to his needs as well as to provide an example of diligence and patriotism to the wives who had followed their husbands to the encampment.

Although the weather that winter was not as severe as first expected, it rained frequently and snowed occasionally. The men kept busy building fortifications, standing guard duty and going on foraging details. None of these jobs came easily. Tools were in short supply, and when it was time for a man to stand guard duty, his fellow cabin mates had to scrounge to come up with one complete outfit for him to wear. Some men went completely naked. Amputations of frozen, blackened limbs was common—without the aid of anesthesia.

Food also was scarce, owing to a poor road system that conspired with the weather to make it difficult for supply wagons to get to Valley Forge. Then there was the problem of money. While the British paid area merchants in gold, the patriots had nearly worthless paper currency to offer. The Americans commonly went for days without tasting meat and only sometimes had salt pork or dried fish to eat. They mainly subsisted on fire cake, a simple mixture of water and cornmeal or wheat flour cooked on a large stone that sat in the middle of an open fire.

The volatile mixture of cold, hunger and poor sanitation led to an outbreak of disease within the encampment. Some soldiers were taken to public hospitals away from Valley Forge, but most chose to stay in their huts surrounded by their friends in spite of the shortage of medical aid.

While Washington inspired his men, the reverse also was true; he gained strength from observing them as well. Their patience and courage in the midst of incredible suffering moved him to write, "Naked and starving as they are we cannot enough admire the incomparable patience and fidelity of the soldiery."[12]

The soldiers at Valley Forge endured the crucible of that terrible winter and emerged stronger, more tempered and ready to face an enemy soft from cozy nights before fires in homes they had commandeered from Philadelphians. The American patriots even made sport of their conditions: "A French volunteer remembered a dinner party to which no one was admitted who possessed a whole pair of trousers."[13]

Still, when conditions reached an intolerable peak in February, the long, dark shadow of despair stretched over the pinnacle of their suffering. Washington realized that something had to give or the fight for independence would be irretrievably lost. What kept the situation from completely deteriorating? Washington's inspired leadership, grounded in a strong Christian faith, was a critical factor. Although many historians contend that he was a deist who believed in a "clockmaker God," one who created the mechanism of the universe, wound it up, then put it exclusively in the hands of men and women, Valley Forge proves otherwise. Stories about Washington during that winter portray a man who believed in a God who actively intervened in human affairs.

One day Isaac Potts, whose home Washington rented at Valley Forge, saw the general's horse tied in an isolated thicket and stopped to investigate. While at a distance, Potts noticed that Washington was on his knees in prayer. The Quaker didn't want to disturb him, so he waited to leave until Washington finished his prayers and rode off on his horse. Potts returned to his wife, telling her, "If George Washington be not a man of God, I am greatly deceived—and still more shall I be deceived, if God do not, through him, work out a great salvation for America."[14]

Yet another incident attests to the depths of Washington's faith. At Valley Forge Michael Wittman's traitorous deeds were uncovered, and he was sentenced to be hanged. The night before, however, an elderly man, Peter Miller, pleaded for the man's clemency to Washington.

The general was adamant. "Impossible!" he said. "Wittman has done all in his power to betray us, even offering to join the British and help destroy us. In these times we cannot be lenient with traitors; and for that reason I cannot pardon your friend."

The white-haired man shook his head. "Friend! He's no friend of mine. He is my bitterest enemy. He has persecuted me for years. He has even beaten me and spit in my face, knowing full well that I would not strike back. Michael Wittman is no friend of mine!"

This perplexed Washington. "And you still wish me to pardon him?"

"I do. I ask it of you as a great personal favor."

"Why?"

"I ask it because Jesus did as much for me."

The general rose from his chair and went to the next room. When he returned, he gave a piece of paper declaring Wittman's pardon to Peter Miller. He told him, "My dear friend, I thank you for this."[15]

In addition to Washington, with his contagious faith and concern for his men, God used another person to lift the soldiers' spirits at Valley Forge and make them into a top-flight army. Friedreich Wilhelm Augustus Baron von Steuben arrived at the end of February at the recommendation of Benjamin Franklin, who was then representing the Americans in Paris. The colorful von Stueben was the son of a Prussian army officer and had himself enlisted at the age of sixteen. Discharged as a captain in 1763, von Steuben could not find a permanent military position in Europe. In America he became the Continental Army's inspector general and quickly rose to the rank of major general.

The intrepid von Stueben spoke little English and had no training manuals with which to work, but that didn't slow him down. His aides worked late for many nights translating into English a manual von Steuben wrote as he went, then made sure each regiment and company had copies by the following day's drill. The Prussian required the hapless soldiers to get into their formations by sunrise each day, teaching them how to use bayonets and maneuver in ranks.

Von Stueben quickly won the men's hearts with his faulty English and his unfailing sense of humor:

> And [he] made the whole thing fun by his ebullient temperament: ecstasy when maneuvers went well, and at mistakes hysterical rages, which the troops came to expect and relish. Drilling with Steuben became the favorite sport at Valley Forge. While engaging in what could almost be a more complicated square dance, the men learned skills that had previously escaped them.[16]

The "invaluable disciplinarian . . . [brought] not only drill but vigor and humor to the thinning and hungry ranks."[17]

Another break for the patriots came as the spring

thaw allowed more supplies of food, clothing and weapons to get to Valley Forge. Other regiments joined them, and new recruits arrived, swelling the ranks to about 20,000. Morale rose. By May the French had rallied to the American cause, joining them in the battle against the British.

In mid-June the continental army successfully engaged the British at the Battle of Monmouth in New Jersey. According to Peter Marshall and David Manuel:

> Historians generally credit Washington as having achieved his greatest feat in holding the army together at Valley Forge. But Washington himself credited God. In announcing the French decision to his joyous troops, he said:
>
> "It having pleased the Almighty Ruler of the universe to defend the cause of the United American States, and finally to raise up a powerful friend among the princes of the earth, to establish our liberty and independence upon a lasting foundation, it becomes us to set apart a day for gratefully acknowledging the divine goodness, and celebrating the important event, which we owe to His divine interposition."[18]

Molly Pitcher

Mary Ludwig Hays McCauley was born on October 13, 1754 near Trenton, New Jersey. History remembers her, however, as "Moll of the Pitcher" or "Molly Pitcher." Following her husband, John, to the Battle of Monmouth, New Jersey, "Molly" carried water to the thirsty troops, who dropped distressingly in the intense summer heat. Her husband, who manned a cannon, also fell victim to heat exhaustion. After tending to him, Molly took his position as cannoneer, which completely startled his artillery mate. She stayed at her post for the duration of the battle, in which the British retreated.

Afterward General George Washington personally thanked Molly for her actions and recommended to the Congress that she receive a sergeant's commission and half-pay for life.[19]

Molly and her husband went to live in Carlisle, Pennsylvania after the war. In 1822, after John's death, she started to receive a $40-a-year pension from the state as a war widow. The Pennsylvania legislature, however, recognized that Molly should receive a pension based on her own war-time heroics. The act that changed the wording read, "for the relief of Molly M'Kolly, for her services during the Revolutionary War."[20]

*   *   *

"Molly Hays watched as her husband John marched off to do battle on that steamy June day in 1778. A sound like a violent thunderclap pierced her ears as other soldiers' wives hastened to safety far behind the lines. Molly lingered, however, and when a cannon boomed, she knew her husband, a sergeant, was at his post.

"Although the patriots weren't about to succumb to the British, many of them faded fast in the 100-degree heat. Molly heard their cries for 'Water! Water!' and realized that if the men were not soon refreshed, the Americans might lose the battle. *We can't lose this fight because our men don't have enough water*, she thought. Without considering her personal safety, Molly rushed to a nearby spring and filled her pail with cold, clear water. Then, hitching up her long, hot skirts, she dashed toward the front, praying she wasn't too late.

"On the battlefield the acrid stench of gunpowder nearly overcame her, but she steadied herself, making trip and after trip from the spring to the dehydrated soldiers. Their throats thick with dust, they opened their mouths like baby birds and drank greedily as Molly poured water into them, beginning with the most urgent cases. As she worked, the young woman tried to keep track of John while he repeatedly shoved a hot ramrod down the cannon's barrel. Only when he slumped over his cannon with heat exhaustion did Molly abandon her trips to the spring.

"She hurried to John's side, took a rag and plunged it into her last pail of water. For several minutes Molly applied the cold compress to his temples, then she helped him into the cannon's shade. Her husband's partner at the canon gaped in amazement as Molly took up the ramrod John had dropped.

" 'Load!' she hollered.

" 'But—' the man stammered.

" 'Load!' Molly insisted.

"When he did so, she thrust the ramrod down the barrel of the cannon. The gunpowder and ammunition fused in an explosive roar, sending black soot all over Molly's sticky clothes. She served as the regiment's cannoneer for the rest of the fight, in spite of fatigue and hands that burned from the blistering ram-rod. The Battle of Monmouth ended in a British re-treat. Molly, who gained the nickname 'Molly Pitcher' that day, lay depleted at her husband's side. Finally a soldier lifted her in his arms and carried Molly to a bed of blankets so she could rest properly from her heroic labors."[3]

John Marshall, Supreme Court Chief Justice—and Every Man

Born in 1755 in the Virginia hinterlands, John Marshall served as a lieutenant in the Revolutionary War and wintered with the troops at Valley Forge. He went on to practice law with only six weeks of formal training under his belt. He became a Virginia legislator, then Secretary of State, and the Supreme Court's third Chief Justice under President John Adams.

Although he was a celebrated American, Marshall was a humble man known for his rumpled personal appearance, as well as his tongue-in-cheek sense of humor. One day as the Chief Justice quietly went about his marketing in Richmond, a stranger approached him with a business proposition.

"Carry this heavy turkey I have just purchased, and I will give you this."

He pressed a coin into Marshall's hand, no doubt thinking himself very generous to be helping this obvi-

ously down-in-the-mouth man. Marshall stuffed the turkey under one arm and meekly padded along behind his benefactor. His friends covered their mouths to prevent their laughter from giving Marshall away.

A fellow justice once said of him, "He was far more anxious to know others, than be known by them."[1] The following incident is a case in point.

* * *

After his antiquated carriage broke down in Winchester, Virginia, Chief Justice Marshall took refuge at a place called McGuire's Hotel. No one knew his identity and never would have guessed it based on his slovenly appearance.

While he relaxed in the tavern, Marshall listened quietly to a few young men argue about Christianity and whether it could be true. Finally one of the men turned and asked him if he had anything to contribute to their discussion, possibly anticipating some ridiculous sentiment from the unkempt figure. Little did they expect the hour-long, eloquent defense of the faith that came from Marshall's lips. No one interrupted the Chief Justice while he spoke or said anything in response when he finished. There really was nothing left to say.

After Marshall left, the men began speculating as to who in the world he could be. The consensus was that only a minister could defend the faith like that. When they later discovered Marshall's true identity, their jaws dropped for the second time that day.

The Trail of Tears

Roughly 13,000 Cherokee Indians began a months-long trek from Georgia to present-day Oklahoma in October 1838. In one sense they followed in the footsteps of other westward adventurers. In another, however, they were very different from their counterparts of European heritage—the Cherokees did not go willingly. One-fourth of them perished as they made their way in the cold months to a strange, new land. Exposure, disease and exhaustion claimed thousands of lives on the journey known as "The Trail of Tears."

How did this happen when the Cherokees, perhaps more than any other Native American tribe, had embraced Christianity and the white culture? In fact, when the removal occurred, their pastors requested that they not have to travel on Sundays so worship services could be held.

The state of Georgia initially acted to remove the Cherokees from the path of white western settlement between 1827-1830. The Native American tribe pledged to adjust to white customs, including taking up farming and ranching. They even formed a constitutional government in northwest Georgia. However, in 1828 the state passed a law declaring all Cherokee laws void and claiming their land. The following years were suspenseful and difficult as the case went to various courts, including the Supreme Court.

The removal of the Cherokees was unjust, ill-conceived and poorly executed; thousands watered the trail west with their tears. Here are two accounts of that ill-fated journey.

* * *

Cherokee chief William Coodey complained in a private letter that most of the Cherokees were forced to leave their homes so quickly that there wasn't time to pack their belongings. Plunderers sacked the houses that weren't sold right out from under their owners at ridiculously low prices.

He wrote:

> Many of the Cherokees, who a few days ago were in comfortable circumstances, are now victims of abject poverty. . . . This is not the description of extreme cases. It is altogether a faint representation of the work which has been perpetuated on the unoffending, unarmed and unresisting Cherokees.[1]

A Maine resident on his way through Kentucky in November and December 1838, observed several contingents of Cherokees, each a day apart. His heart went out to them, especially the elderly, who seemed to be suffering the most from the miserable journey. All of them looked tired, and many were obviously ill as they tried to stay upright ten miles a day along frozen ground in one area and muddy streets in another, barefooted. The eyewitness learned that at every stop the Cherokees routinely buried fourteen or fifteen of their members.

In their faces he saw dejection and near-despair. Among some of the Cherokees he noticed a certain wildness that, if encouraged, he thought might lead to violence against the white soldiers who guarded them like criminals. He wept as he prayed for them, wondering how such a thing could happen in the United States of America.

By the time the Cherokees completed their tragic trek, one out of four was dead.

The Abolitionists

The movement to abolish slavery gained important ground in the 1830s as opponents of the system produced their own newspapers and spoke out in various forums against that immoral institution. It was a polarizing crusade, however, and its adherents faced enormous public censure, personal ridicule and danger. Rotten eggs and the noise of tin horns, drums and sleigh bells often assaulted them as they made public addresses.

In Philadelphia abolitionists who built an assembly hall watched an angry mob burn it to the ground shortly thereafter. In fact, violence against abolitionists raged throughout the northern states. In one Maine village a man built a school for black children only to discover it in the middle of a swamp upon its completion. Irate farmers had dragged it there the previous night with their teams of oxen.

Newspaper editor William Lloyd Garrison was attacked by a so-called "broadcloth mob" that put a rope around his neck and led him through the streets of Boston. That same day in Utica, New York, a mob of "very respectable gentlemen," including a judge and a congressman, disrupted the organizational meeting of an abolitionist group.

One event more than any other, however, energized the abolitionist cause nationwide. It prompted the creation of nearly a thousand antislavery societies in the northern states, elevating the movement in the public's mind from extremism to respectability.

Elijah Lovejoy

In 1837 a highly respected, Princeton-trained minister and newspaper editor pleaded with the citizens of Alton, Illinois to protect his constitutional right to freedom of the press. Elijah Lovejoy had edited *The Observer*, a weekly abolitionist paper in St. Louis, until pro-slavery renegades destroyed his printing press, threatened his family, and ran him out of town. From there the thirty-five-year-old Lovejoy ventured to Illinois where he established that state's antislavery society and continued printing *The Observer*.

The minister did not find peace, however, in Alton. Night after night his family huddled fearfully inside their home as angry crowds threatened to burn down the house and kill its occupants.

At the start of November, 1837 the Reverend Lovejoy appeared at a public meeting in the Alton courtroom to defend his abolitionist convictions and appeal for personal protection from violence and his right to freedom of the press. He moved many to tears as he described the hardships he faced night after night as he and a few dozen supporters guarded his family and his printing press.

Lovejoy stood confidently before the chairman of the public meeting where he initially defended his abolitionist position and actions. It wasn't true, he insisted, that he ran an antislavery press or made speeches simply to provoke Alton's citizens, or that he deliberately flew in the face of convention just to be different or to incite civil disorder. No, he said, he stood where he did on slavery because of strongly held convictions:

> But, sir, while I value the good opinion of my fellow-citizens as highly as anyone, I may be permitted to say that I am governed by higher considerations than either the favour or fear of man. I am impelled to the course I have taken because I fear God. As I shall answer it to my God in the great day, I dare not abandon my sentiments, or cease in all proper ways to propagate them.[1]

The refined and appealing minister also asserted that he wasn't addressing the public assembly in order to compromise his beliefs. Rather, all he wanted was the personal protection and freedom of the press afforded him under the United States Constitution. While his only "crime" was offending some people's sentiments regarding slavery, Lovejoy insisted that he had broken no laws. He didn't deserve to be "hunted down continually like a partridge" or threatened with being tarred and feathered. "Why am I waylaid every day," he asked, "and from night to night, and my life in jeopardy every hour?"

The main issue facing them, he said, was whether he could enjoy his constitutional rights. Would he and his long-suffering family and their property be protected from lawless individuals who didn't approve of his beliefs?

As the minister told how his ailing wife fled to the attic from her sickbed almost nightly to escape mobs with brickbats surrounding their home, he started to weep. Many in the Alton courtroom sobbed as well, moved by his deep concern for her. Even some of his enemies cried.

"Forgive me, sir, that I have thus betrayed a weakness," Lovejoy said after regaining his composure. "It was the allusion to my family that overcame my feelings. Not, sir, I assure you, from any fears on my part. I have no personal fears."[2]

But what was he to do, he asked, if the town of Alton didn't offer some protection from pro-slavery agitators? It was not as if he could leave and find a more tolerant community. He had tried that route before; in fact, he had brought his family to Alton looking for refuge. Besides, Lovejoy had no guarantee that he and his family would be able to leave Alton without being overtaken enroute by ruffians.

No, he had made up his mind after consulting with family, friends and God to stand fast and "to insist on protection in the exercise of my rights." He was, he said, even prepared to die for his convictions, if need be. "If the civil authorities refuse to protect me," he concluded, "I must look to God;

and if I die, I have determined to make my grave in Alton."[3]

* * *

On the night of November 7 many who participated in that town meeting descended upon the warehouse where Lovejoy and about fifteen men defended his fourth printing press. Pro-slavery gunslingers fired twice into the building; Lovejoy and his defenders fired back, knowing that the law would not be on their side. Then the mob set fire to the warehouse, and as Lovejoy fled, his enemies shot him to death. Afterward they dragged his mangled body through the streets of Alton.

Public outrage greeted the news of Lovejoy's martyrdom. There had been other abolitionists who surrendered their lives for the cause, but none had touched the American spirit as that respectable, gentle and forsaken minister. This was no extremist, but a man to whom freedom-loving Americans could relate.

Lovejoy's death moved Massachusetts senator Henry Wilson to reflect:

> Nothing had so clearly indicated to antislavery men the nature of the conflict in which they were engaged, the desperate character of the foe with which they were grappling. . . . They saw that the conflict was not to be the bloodless encounter of ideas.[4]

Abolitionist and feminist Sarah Grimké prophetically told a friend there was little hope now that slavery could be stopped peacefully. She said, "The blood spilled at Alton will be seed of the future discord."[5]

Shortly after Lovejoy's murder his brother Owen traveled to churches throughout Ohio to tell the story of what had happened at Alton. People wept as they heard about the minister who had courageously defended his rights, not for selfish purposes, but to free and empower black men and women.

At one church a man stood in the back after listening to Owen Lovejoy's stirring message. He raised his right hand and proclaimed before the congregation, "Here, before God, in the presence of these witnesses, I consecrate my life to the destruction of slavery." His name was John Brown.[6]

The Moses of Her People

In the years before the Civil War abolitionists created a secret network—an "underground railroad"—to rescue slaves in the South. A clandestine movement which used the imagery of a passenger train to describe its operations, the Underground Railroad was a cluster of people who put their lives on the line to rescue blacks from their owners because they believed that "all men are created equal."

Although the actual number of slaves who escaped was tiny, the "railroad" provided an important psychological boost to supporters of the abolitionist movement, not to mention the people who found freedom through it.

Conducting an escape was very dangerous; slave owners relentlessly pursued their "property" and had the law on their side—even in the northern states, thanks to the Fugitive Slave Acts of 1793 and 1850. But that didn't discourage the most famous of the "conductors," an illiterate former slave named Harriet Tubman. After she escaped from bondage in Maryland's eastern shore, Tubman repeatedly returned south to guide more than 300 slaves to freedom, taking some as far as Canada. This story describes one of her risky forays for freedom.

*   *   *

Eleven runway slaves jumped at the sound of urgently barking dogs nearby. Their owners were hot on the trail, threatening to overtake them. Harriet Tubman's presence steadied the fugitives. At just five feet tall, this sturdy, strong-willed ex-slave hurried her frightened charges into a frigid stream. She knew from experience that even in daylight they would be safe because the dogs couldn't pick up their scent in the water. Her sharpened instincts proved her right again. When that danger died down, Harriet furtively led the runaway slaves to one of the farms along the Underground Railroad.

When the small group finally reached the appointed farmhouse, a stranger came to the door, eyeing Harriet warily. She asked for the man who had helped her before, only to learn that he had fled after the authorities had found him out. Harriet hurried back to the runaways, who anxiously waited for her in the woods. She knew that it would be only a matter of time before the new owner squealed on her.

They rushed ahead, feet aching and stomachs rumbling. All they had eaten for days were wild berries, corn, apples and an occasional fish when they had the time to catch them in the streams they passed.

Harriet Tubman encouraged the frightened runaways not to give up. She had been through hard journeys before and knew her way around fear and danger. They had total confidence in her. Wasn't she the Moses of her people, leading blacks to freedom as the Bible hero had led the Jews out of their Egyptian bondage centuries before?

Actually, one of the runaways wasn't so sure about her. When he stated his intention to go back, Harriet forbade it. Chances were good that he would be caught and forced to give up their position under duress. When the man insisted, Harriet resorted to the one argument she reserved for situations like this. She pulled a gun out of her coat and stated unequivocally, "Live North or die here." The man decided to live North.

One terrible day, however, it seemed they would never make it to that promised land. Harriet led them to a murky, foul-smelling swamp, explaining as they crept gingerly into the tall grasses that Underground Railroad workers often passed by there to offer help. Why the swamp? It was so awful that no one else would go near it.

As night fell, Harriet and her runaways shivered in the darkness. Suddenly they heard a man's voice, and their hearts pounded in fear and anticipation. The stranger muttered, "My wagon stands in the barnyard across the way." He also informed them that his horse was ready to go, and that there was plenty of food and blankets for everyone.

A little while later, Harriet ran a reconnaissance mission to the barn and found everything just as the man had said. When she returned to the others, she joyfully reported that the tide had turned, and they were on the way to freedom. "Praise God!" they cried.[7]

Sojourner Truth: Preacher-Abolitionist

"Isabella" was born some time in the late 1790's in Ulster County, New York, a state that emancipated its slaves in 1827. At that time Isabella went to New York City and found work as a domestic servant. She also joined the African Methodist Episcopal Church and began preaching at evangelistic services led by Elijah Pierson, who first recognized that she had a compelling gift for speaking.

By 1843 Isabella had decided to change her name because:

> I wasn't goin' to keep nothin' of Egypt on me, an' so I went to the Lord an' asked him to give me a new name. And the Lord gave me Sojourner, because I was to travel up an' down the land, showin' the people their sins, an' bein' a sign unto them. Afterwards I told the Lord I wanted another name, 'cause everybody else had two names; and the Lord gave me Truth, because I was to declare the truth to the people.[8]

Sojourner Truth became an itinerant evangelist who also promoted abolition for her people in the South, as well as women's suffrage. A powerful speaker, she could

not read or write. Although she led many people to faith in Christ, needless to say, her efforts were not always appreciated.

* * *

"Break up this here meeting, or we'll set fire to your tents!" shouted a large crowd of white men as Sojourner Truth, ex-slave and itinerant preacher, waited for her turn to speak at a Massachusetts camp meeting in 1844.

A white female minister was about to begin her message when the mob appeared and issued its threat. Sojourner watched in fear and trembling as the speaker stood wide-eyed and scared. Realizing that she was the only black person in the meeting, Sojourner hurried to a corner of a tent where she cringed behind a trunk. What might the mob of angry young men do if they got hold of her? Her cowardice was short-lived, however. Sojourner was a woman of faith and knew what she had to do.

She went outside and climbed to the top of a hill overlooking the crowd. Gathering all her courage, knowing that Jesus was with her, she raised her voice in a powerful song:

It was early in the morning,
It was early in the morning,
Just at the break of day,
When He rose,
When He rose,
When He rose,
And went to heaven on a cloud.

Both the rioters and the worshipers gazed incredulously at Sojourner as they took in her powerful, resolute voice. Yet the black woman's worst fears came true when the protesters suddenly dashed toward her. She saw that most of them were carrying sticks and clubs as they surrounded her on all sides.

When the men closed in, Sojourner stopped singing. Then she asked, "Why do you come about me with clubs and sticks? I am not doing harm to anyone."

To which several men replied, 'We ain't goin' to hurt you, old woman. We just came to hear you sing!'[2]

A Great Awakening
for Theodore Weld

I n the early part of the nineteenth century, a Second Great Awakening swept through the country.
This movement of God's Spirit placed less empha-
sis on man's depravity and predestination and more
on the individual's decision to follow Christ, his or her
subsequent holiness and reforming society's ills than
the first one before the Revolution. Charles Finney, a
Connecticut lawyer who was converted in 1821, was
his era's greatest preacher and the Second Great
Awakening's chief figure.

Enormously popular, Finney still had his detrac-
tors. One eloquent student at Hamilton College in
New York, the son of a respected clergyman, held
him in almost legendary derision. Theodore Weld
sneered at Finney's lack of formal theological training, as well as his emotionally oriented revival meetings. He repeatedly criticized the evangelist to his
fellow students.

Hamilton was near the hub of Finney's ministry in Utica, and one day Weld went there to visit his favorite aunt. His friends couldn't wait to find out what Theodore would do if he found himself in the despised Finney's company.

* * *

Weld's aunt had been concerned about his spiritual condition for some time. After all, growing up as a pastor's son doesn't automatically usher a person into the kingdom of God. On the Sunday of Theodore's visit, his aunt decided to take him to hear Charles Finney preach. She knew, however, that he loathed Finney, that he had said he never wanted to get anywhere near the wretched revivalist. She simply made sure that Theodore didn't find out who was preaching that day and then scrunched him into a pew with relatives like book ends on either side to prevent his escape once he found out.

Finney had heard that a young man who detested his ministry would be in attendance that morning. He preached powerfully about the harm that a gifted and influential person could do by coming out on the wrong side of Jesus Christ. Weld started to squirm. As Finney continued preaching on "One sinner destroyeth much good," Theodore rose. Seeing her nephew's rattled condition and his intention to leave, his aunt blocked the way by leaning forward in prayer.

Although Theodore sat back down out of respect for her, he tried again to break out when the hard-hitting message got too close to home. His aunt remained unmovable, though, like Gibraltar. In silent resignation, Weld banged angrily against the pew, crossed his arms against his chest and glared at the man who "toasted me on the prongs of his fork," as Weld put it later.

The following day Weld got his revenge when, to his surprise, he bumped into Finney at a shop in town. Now he would give the rotten evangelist a taste of his own lousy medicine.

"Do you know what it's like to sit like a prisoner in a pew while someone takes jabs at you, and there's nothing you can do about it?" Weld screamed and stormed at Finney, attracting a crowd. "Men like you should be strung up and left to rot for the birds."

On and on he went, using his powerful voice and some choice language, while Finney stood silently. A crowd quickly gathered around them, gaping at the scene. After some time, Weld finally ran out of steam.

"Mr. Weld," Finney said, "are you the son of a minister of Christ? And is this the way for you to behave?"

For once, Theodore didn't have an answer. He turned on his heel and left the store, forgetting his reason for going there in the first place. For the next hour he wrestled like Jacob with God, a session which ended with Weld's knock on Finney's door. He apologized for his offensive behavior, and the evangelist forgave him, then offered to pray with the young man. Weld complied.

At Finney's next service a day later he looked up to find the once angry young man standing and facing him. "May I please speak?" Weld asked humbly. Finney gave his permission. Before the people of Utica, Weld apologized for his behavior, professed Christ and asked for the people's forgiveness.

Not only did the assembly receive Weld gladly into their hearts, but Finney asked the young man to stay on, to use his gift of public speaking for God's glory. Theodore left Hamilton College and threw himself into the movement he had ridiculed, for the sake of the God he had come to know personally. He went on to become one of America's leading abolitionists.[1]

The Civil War

ollowing Abraham Lincoln's election in 1860, the Southern states began to secede from the Union in spite of the president-elect's promise to respect slavery where it existed. Southerners feared that his pledge would not last. In addition, the agrarian South's determination not to let the economically wealthier and technologically more advanced North dominate it or change its lifestyle contributed to secession. In a sense, the Civil War was a struggle between the medieval idea of chivalry transplanted in a democratic society and the aggressively modern world with its dizzying industrial power.

However, the central issue in sectional conflicts remained that of slavery. In the 1850s much impassioned debate had occurred over the spread of that institution to the new western territories and whether those places had a right to have slaves or not.

In 1860 Lincoln ran as an antislavery Republican against two Democrats, Stephen Douglas, who favored a territory's right to choose slavery, and John C.

Breckinridge, a pro-slavery candidate. Within weeks of Lincoln's election, South Carolina became the first Southern state to secede. Six others followed in February, 1861. (Four slave states, Maryland, Delaware, Missouri and Kentucky, remained within the Union.) That same month a new government was formed: the Confederate States of America, with Jefferson Davis as its president.

In Lincoln's inaugural speech in March he called upon the South to compromise, promising that the federal government would not interfere with "the domestic institutions of the states." War was, he said, up to them. In response Southern forces began seizing ports, custom houses and post offices in their region. When a United States officer requested reinforcements to keep Fort Sumter in South Carolina under Federal control, the Confederates asked him to surrender, then fired the first shots of the Civil War.

Initially most people believed the conflict wouldn't last long, especially since the North had superior numbers, industrial resources, and a strong central government. However, the War between the States claimed more American lives than any other in which our nation has participated. Out of a population of 35 million, 620,000 men lost their lives with at least that many wounded—364,000 from the North and 258,000 from the South. The war also led to great physical destruction in the South; nevertheless, it cemented the Union and brought about the freeing of almost 4 million blacks.

The United States Christian Commission

The United States Christian Commission (USCC) was a wartime relief agency established in November 1861. It promoted the spiritual and physical health of Northern troops in a myriad of ways, including the distribution of Christian tracts and New Testaments. USCC members also led prayer meetings, conducted worship services and assisted the wounded and ill in hospitals and in the field. At the conclusion of a battle, USCC delegates often arrived first on the scene with supplies and support.

They also established "Special Diet Kitchens" for the wounded whose digestive systems weren't up to regular food, inspected sanitary conditions in camps and sent lists of casualties to their home bases. The commission helped soldiers send their pay home, provided accommodations and transportation for family members to visit their sick and dying, and helped pay for the transport of soldiers' bodies in the event of death.

Their work didn't stop even at that point. USCC members read to soldiers, wrote letters for them and established a portable library for the wounded and sick. Also through USCC influence, many officers volunteered to teach reading and math to and black soldiers.

For assistance with its work the USCC established a network of roughly 10,000 Northern churches and relief agencies who made and collected clothes, food and medical supplies. By war's end, the United States Christian Commission had collected and distributed over $6 million in supplies and money.

The following are some accounts of USCC activities during the War between the States.

* * *

One wounded solider saw "the shadow of a man carrying a lantern in his hand." Every so often the man would stoop down, then he would move a short distance further and stoop again. The solider quickly realized that the man was elevating the heads of his wounded comrades to give them a drink. So much did he want some water that he began praying earnestly that the shadowy form would include him on his round of mercy. He tried to cry out to get the man's attention, but he was so parched that nothing would come out. As the man of mercy neared, the soldier thrashed his arm about to get his attention. "In a moment more," the soldier said, "he was kneeling by my side and pouring what, I thought, was heaven, down my throat."[1]

* * *

A USCC delegate working in Virginia came upon a pathetic sight one steamy July day. Lying on the second floor of a sweltering barn just under its roof, sixty-five wounded soldiers suffered in the intense heat. The USCC man gave them something to eat, then asked the soldier who was nursing them to please wash the men's hands and feet to relieve their distress. The soldier regarded the Christian worker disdainfully. "I did not enlist to wash men's feet," he said. "Bring me the water, then, and I will do it," came the response. The soldier brought him the water, and the USCC delegate gladly bathed each of the sixty-five soldiers' hands and feet.[2]

*   *   *

When George Greedy of Bucks County, Pennsylvania left for the battlefield, he took a pocket New Testament with him, a gift from a group of USCC ladies. He knew the inscriptions they had written by heart, from Psalm 91:11, "He shall give his angels charge over thee, to keep thee in all thy ways," and First Timothy 6:12, "Fight the good fight."

During his time of service, Greedy fought at the battle of White Oak Swamp where he narrowly escaped death. A bullet shattered his left arm and went through his coat where it split his New Testament from Revelation to the eleventh chapter of John. The bullet finally came to rest after slightly wounding Greedy in the stomach.

He told a USCC field delegate at his hospital that he would have been killed had it not been for that New Testament in his breast pocket. When the delegate asked to borrow the book to show some USCC people, Greedy gave his consent. He added, however, "I would never sell it, for it saved my life."[3]

Religious Awakening on the Rapidan

There are many stories of revivals among fighting men during the Civil War. This one comes via Confederate General John B. Gordon, who participated in all the campaigns of the Army of Northern Virginia, finishing the war commanding half of Robert E. Lee's army. He wrote about the spiritual revival among his troops in a book published in 1903, a year before his death.

* * *

General Gordon and his men passed the winter of 1863-64 on the banks of Virginia's Rapidan River near Clark's Mountain, preparing for the harsh Battle of the Wilderness that would come in May. He recalled watching Robert E. Lee survey the white-tented Union army below through his field glasses. For several months both armies passed the quiet days in unexpected, welcome peace.

Among the Confederate troops the busiest people were the chaplains who, along with ministers visiting from nearby places, prepared altars for the soldiers in their ragged uniforms to worship and pray. "The religious revivals that ensued," said Gordon, "form a most remarkable and impressive chapter of war history."[4]

The soldiers met for worship not just on Sundays, but throughout the week for hours at a time. Indeed, the services continued for several weeks with impressive attendance until, as the General recorded, "they brought under religious influence the great body of the army."[5]

Gordon recalled how the very rocks and trees echoed thousands of men's praises and petitions and how those men went on to follow Jesus all the days of their lives, no matter how brief or long. A committed Christian himself, General Lee encouraged the revivals because he maintained a strong interest in his men's spiritual welfare.

God's Humble Instrument

On April 2, 1865, with the war in its twilight, Abraham Lincoln toured the decimated Confederate capital of Richmond, Virginia with a small entourage. The reception given Lincoln by a group of the city's newly freed blacks moved Admiral D.D. Porter, who was with the President. This incident occurred less than two weeks before the President's assassination.

* * *

That the war finally was over heartened Abraham Lincoln. He told his companions on the way to see Richmond that it was like dreaming a terrible dream for four years and at last waking from it.

Admiral Porter remembered landing along the riverbank and surveying the city's deserted streets. The only people in sight were a dozen blacks digging with spades near a small house. Their leader, a man of about sixty, quickly dropped his spade and hurried over to President Lincoln.

"Bless the Lord!" he cried in a thick Southern dialect, falling on his knees and kissing the great man's feet. "Here is the great Messiah!" With these and other exclamations he welcomed the President, as his companions followed suit.

Lincoln was visibly shaken by the greeting and pleaded with the men to get up. "Don't kneel to me," he said. "That is not right. You must kneel to God only, and thank Him for the liberty you will hereafter enjoy. I am but God's humble instrument.

"You may rest assured," he continued, "that as long as I live no one shall put a shackle to your limbs, and you shall have all the rights which God has given to every other free citizen of this Republic."

Admiral Porter described Lincoln's face as otherworldly, full of kindness and grace. With some reluctance he was able to convince them to rise and leave the President. "The scene was so touching that I hated to disturb it," he said, "yet we could not stay there all day."

The man in charge of the work crew understood. As he broke away from the President he told Porter, "After bein' so many years in the desert without water, it's mighty pleasant to be lookin' at last on our spring of life."

Before allowing Lincoln to withdraw, however, the men joined hands and sang from their hearts:

Oh, all ye people clap your hands,
    And with triumphant voices sing;
No force the mighty power withstands
    Of God, the universal King.

"The President and all of us listened respectfully while the hymn was being sung," Porter recalled. Then, to his amazement, Richmond's streets suddenly filled with newly freed black men, women and children. Some hurried over to Lincoln to touch him, while others stood gaping in awe from a respectful distance. Porter watched a few turn somersaults. Many were yelling for joy. Lincoln couldn't just stand there; he had to address them.

As he lifted his voice, a hush fell upon the crowd as they strained to catch every word:

My poor friends, you are free—free as air. You can cast off the name of slave and trample upon it; it will come to you no more. Liberty is your birthright. God gave it to you as He gave it to others, and it is a sin that you have been deprived of it for so many years. But you must try to deserve this priceless boon. Let the world see that you merit it, and are able to maintain it by your good works. Don't let your joy carry you into excesses. Learn the laws and obey them; obey God's commandments and thank Him for giving you liberty; for to Him you owe all things. There, now, let me pass on; I have but little time to spare. I want to see the capital, and must return at once to Washington to secure to you that liberty which you seem to prize so highly.[6]

The Gettysburg Address

On November 19, 1863 President Lincoln spoke at the dedication of the Gettysburg National Cemetery to commemorate the horrific battle that had taken place there. Starting on July 1 of that year, 75,000 Confederate troops had clashed with 85,000 Union soldiers. The Southern forces under Robert E. Lee retreated in defeat, but only after both sides had suffered heavy losses.

For two solid hours at the cemetery's dedication, the famous statesman and orator Edward Everett waxed eloquent about the significance of the Gettysburg battle. When he finished, Lincoln ambled to the podium with his own humble little speech, one that merited only the inside pages of the next day's newspapers.

Everett, however, recognized the speech's great significance. He was moved to write Lincoln, "I wish that I could flatter myself that I had come as near to the central idea of the occasion in two hours as you did in two minutes."

* * *

Fourscore and seven years ago our fathers brought forth on this continent, a new nation, conceived in liberty, and dedicated to the proposition that all men are created equal.

Now we are engaged in a great civil war, testing whether that nation or any nation so conceived and so dedicated, can long endure. We are met on a great battlefield of that war. We have come to dedicate a portion of that field as a final resting place for those who here gave their lives that that nation might live. It is altogether fitting and proper that we should do this.

But, in a larger sense, we cannot dedicate—we cannot consecrate—we cannot hallow—this ground. The brave men, living and dead, who struggled here, have consecrated it, far above our poor power to add or detract. The world will little note, nor long remember what we say here, but it can never forget what they did here. It is for us the living, rather, to be dedicated here to the unfinished work which they who fought here have thus far so nobly advanced. It is rather for us to be here dedicated to that cause for which they gave the last full measure of devotion—that we take increased devotion to that cause for which they gave the last full measure of devotion—that we here highly resolve that these dead shall not have died in vain—that this nation, under God, shall have a new birth of freedom—and that government of the people, by the people, for the people, shall not perish from the earth.[7]

Lee's Surrender to Grant

President Lincoln's second inaugural address in March 1865 set the tone for the coming aftermath of the Civil War:

With malice toward none; with charity for all; with firmness in the right, as God gives us to see the right, let us strive on to finish the work we are in; to bind up the nation's wounds; to care for him who shall have borne the battle, and for his widow, and his orphan—to do all which may achieve and cherish a just, and a lasting peace, among ourselves, and with all nations.[8]

In that conciliatory spirit General Ulysses S. Grant accepted the surrender of his Confederate counterpart, Robert E. Lee, at Appomattox Court House in Virginia on April 9, 1865. Eyewitness Lloyd Lewis described the scene.

* * *

"It was strangely quiet even for Sunday, this ninth day of April, 1865, as Ulysses S. Grant jogged along the Virginia road that led to Appomattox Court House, his head drooping on his stubby little body.

"The big guns were still. Through the woods on either side of the white road, two armies sat motionless, waiting.

"One of them was his, the bruised but powerful Army of the Potomac, the other was that of his enemies, the Army of Northern Virginia, bled white and exhausted.

"Grant, always solemn, more solemn now than ever, was riding to receive Robert E. Lee's surrender, and it made him sad. At Lee . . . and at [his] desperate Army

of Northern Virginia, last hope of the South, he had been pounding all spring, all the winter before, and the summer before that. Now the end had come. He was glad it was over, but compassion for the brave old foe drowned all the elation of his own triumph. . . .

"Into a two-story brick house on the edge of a tiny village he went as to his own surrender, dust and ashes over his mussy uniform, a private's stained overcoat upon his back, looking, as he entered, like a Missouri farmer who had by mistake crawled into a blouse that carried, unnoticed, three little silver stars on its shoulders.

"Awaiting him was Lee, who of all men knew that those stars were no mistake, Lee in his own resplendent uniform, handsome, aristocratic, perfect model of the old army manners and professional culture to which both Grant and he had been trained at West Point—ideals which he had remembered and which Grant, luckily for the Union, had so soon forgotten.

"The aristocrat wore a sword, the democrat none, and, noticing this, the democrat, with a grave courtesy that somehow shamed the lofty hauteur of the cavalier, explained that he had not had time to bring out his official blade and get fixed up for the ceremony.

"As simply and naturally as though at an ordinary meeting of officers, Grant presented his staff, and the Union men, admiring the great Confederate, made gracious attempts to ease the situation with small, pleasant talk. But to them Lee, who had been an officer all his life, could be only stiff and cool, and when his eye fell on Grant's military secretary, Colonel Ely S. Parker, full-bloodied Indian chief of the Six Nations, he stared in amazement, evidently thinking that the Yankees had brought in a Negro officer to humiliate him.

"But under the gentle voice of his plain, slouching conqueror, Lee's proud reserve began to thaw. Grant talked of the Mexican War, in which both had served, and would have gone on in such informal fashion if Lee had not brought up the business of that day—surrender.

"Grant silently wrote out the terms. They were simple: the enlisted men were to surrender their arms, the officers to retain theirs, all were to give their paroles and go home, not to be disturbed by United States authority so long as they kept their promise not to fight the government again. He handed them to his adversary and waited. Lee wiped his glasses, adjusted them to his nose and began reading.

"The sweeping generosity of the terms, considering what the Southern politicians had told their soldiers about the bloodthirst of the North, must have been plain in their full significance to Lee.

"His face lit up when he came to the clause which allowed the officers to keep their property, and when he had finished he said with a little ring in his voice, 'This will have a very happy effect upon my army.'

"Grant wanted the whole thing to be happy and asked if Lee had anything more to suggest. The Confederate wondered if his cavalrymen and artillerymen, who owned their horses, would be permitted to keep them. 'No, the terms as written don't permit it,' said Grant. He hadn't known the Southern army was thus organized. But he would allow it anyway and do better than that, he said; he would tell his officers to let every man claim a horse or mule and take it home.

The Confederate privates were mostly small farmers, that he knew, and with their land overrun by two armies they would find times hard, indeed, without work horses.

"At this Lee melted entirely.

" 'This will have the best possible effect upon the men,' he said, warming to so unmartial a conquistador. 'It will be very gratifying and will do much toward conciliating our people.'

"Then as staff officers copied the letters of surrender and the terms, Lee bent toward Grant, as in embarrassment, and whispered in his rival's ear that his men hadn't had anything but parched corn to eat in several days. It was like one brother confiding in another. Grant turned to his staff officers; 'You go to the Twenty-fourth, you to the Fiftieth,' and so on, naming his various corps, 'and ask every man who has three rations to turn over two of them. Go to the commissaries, go to the quartmasters. General Lee's army is on the point of starvation.'

"Away rode the officers and Lee's men received the food, which they wanted, almost as soon as the news of the surrender which, exhausted though they were, they did not want.

"Through the Union lines went the word like a spring wind. Guns began to boom salutes of victory. Grant, hearing them, ordered all celebrations to stop. 'The rebels are our countrymen again; the best sign of rejoicing after the victory will be to abstain from all demonstrations on the field,' he said.

"Grant rode one way, Lee the other, such a sight as the world never saw before, the victor as depressed as the vanquished. Around Lee pressed his ragged starvelings, weeping, holding his hand, calling upon God to bless him. He wept, too, saying, 'I have done the best I could for you.' "[9]

The Frontier Life

Following the American Revolution the western boundary of the United States lay at the Mississippi River. A land rush broke out after the War of 1812, when Indian resistance to western settlement started to break. By 1860 the "frontier line" ran through Wisconsin, Minnesota, Iowa, Nebraska, Kansas, and Texas, with fully half of the country's 31.5 million people living west of the Appalachian Mountains.

A major reason that people moved west was cheap land. In the east, available properties were becoming harder and more expensive to obtain for the average family. The fertile lands of the west also attracted immigrants who came to America seeking freedom and the opportunity to improve their lot in life. In the early 1800s, for example, just $100 would buy a farm in the western territories.

Life was difficult. Pioneers were largely responsible for their own defense since initially there were few jails. A settler learned to work with a rifle at his or her side. A horse thief paid with his life since the loss of an animal could destroy a person's financial well-being. Often settlers lived at great distances from their nearest neighbors.

Daily life on the frontier also involved dawn-to-dusk work, with recreation and intellectual pursuits coming only after a family's needs were met. Revivals brought an exuberant Christianity to the pioneers, whose only two books were usually the Bible and *Pilgrim's Progress*. Those people had to develop a strong sense of independence and self-reliance to survive and, in the process, influenced the character not only of the American West, but of the nation at large.

In the 1930s Laura Ingalls Wilder began to reflect on her own childhood on the western prairies in the closing years of the nineteenth century. Frontier life was becoming a hazy memory for most Americans by then, and she decided to write children's books based on her remembrances of growing up in the days of cowboys, Indians and burgeoning railroads. Her ten *Little House on the Prairie* books became classics. After World War II General Douglas Mac-Arthur requested that they be translated into German and Japanese so the children of those nations could learn more about what had made America so great.

* * *

Thirteen-year-old Laura Ingalls strained to read her school book in the half-hearted light of day. The blizzard of 1880-81 raged outside as if nature had pulled a shade on the sun.

"Ma, couldn't I please go out for a few minutes?" Laura begged. Bored and restless, she'd been cooped up for days. Although she read, sang and memorized Bible verses to pass the time, the teenager yearned to stretch her muscles and breathe fresh air.

"No one is going outside in this, young lady," Caroline Ingalls spoke sternly. She knew about people who, during other blizzards, had frozen to death between their barns and their cabins due to poor visibility.

Laura sighed. "May I at least have a little more kerosene for the lamp, then?"

"I'm sorry, Laura," her mother said gently. She hated to keep saying no. "We have to conserve everything."

Charles Ingalls nodded. "We can't keep the snow off the tracks long enough for the trains to get through with supplies. I've also just heard that the stores in town are running out of everything. We have to make all our reserves last if . . ." He didn't add the last part of the sentence: "if we're going to survive." Everyone knew what he meant.

Fiendish blizzards lashed DeSmet in the Dakota Territory all winter long, creating snow drifts that rose to forty feet. No one went to school or church. The trains didn't make it in time to bring material Christmas cheer, but the tiny community quietly celebrated their vital faith in God, a faith that sustained them until May, when the first trains finally made it through.[1]

Combatting Demon Rum

The nineteenth century was an age of reform. Largely middle-class Christians took up causes from religious instruction for orphans to improving inhumane prisons and mental institutions, opening special schools for the blind and deaf, protesting slavery and promoting women's suffrage. These crusades and the people behind them created a momentum that persisted throughout the century.

Of all the reforms, the most widely supported was the temperance movement, which came into being to combat the widespread drunkenness of that era; people often began drinking hard cider at breakfast. By 1820 the per capita consumption of hard liquor had reached a peak of five gallons per year, the highest it has ever been in American history.

Above and beyond the social costs of drinking was its spiritual cost. Evangelist Charles Finney claimed that alcohol kept many a soul from Christ.

In 1826 the American Temperance Union formed to convince the public that drinking led to criminal acts, accidents, relationship problems, and illness. It advocated the practice of civil disobedience in order to eliminate drunkenness. It also fostered the questionable notion that women were morally superior to men, that their hearts were purer and, therefore, their prayers on behalf of decency and order had more clout with God.

Despite its unorthodox views, temperance had its effect. Maine passed the first effective law prohibiting the manufacture and sale of alcohol in 1851, and by 1855 the per capita consumption of hard liquor had dropped 60 percent.

Although women are largely remembered for fueling the temperance movement, many men effectively stormed the bastion of drink as well, including Dr. Dio Lewis, who lectured throughout the country on "The Influence of Christian Women in the Temperance Cause." Lewis told how his mother rallied her church's women to convince the local saloon keeper to shut down his operation.

During an 1873 speech in Fredonia, New York, Lewis compelled his audience of married couples to march on their hotel's bar. The man in charge swore that he never drank and would stop selling liquor if the pharmacist across the street would also comply. According to one historian, "By nightfall they had brought the druggist to his knees."[1] Such scenes were repeated wherever Lewis lectured, encouraging the movement that came to be known as the Women's Crusade.

The most famous of the movement's champions, however, was Miss Francis Willard, who became president of the Women's Christian Temperance Union and America's heroine for the latter part of that energetic century.

* * *

It was a biting cold night with a zero wind rushing across Lake Michigan. The street was mostly deserted but there was a sound of a distant singing of a hymn. . . . [The Rev. John B. Gough's] curiosity was roused. Around the corner, in the snow, under a flickering street lamp, knelt twenty-five or thirty women. Before them was a notorious saloon. They had been chanting the 146th Psalm.

As John came to pause beside a policeman a few feet away, one of the women began to pray.

"There they go again," groaned the officer. "McGuire had them enjoined from blocking his sidewalk yesterday and since dawn today they've knelt in the gutter. 'Git 'em away from here or I gits your star,' says McGuire. 'How can I git 'em away?' says I. They's ladies, every one of 'em. I can't lay hands on 'em like I could some hussy from Water Street."

"The Woman's Crusade!" John exclaimed. "So it's reached Chicago! Who'd have thought it! What can they hope to do here?"

"They've closed fifteen saloons in a week already; that's what they can do," replied the officer. Just then the door swung open and a tall man in an apron shouted, "Get the blank out of here, ye blank . . ."

"Here, that won't do!" John said, as he took a step forward. But the policeman held him.

"They brought it on themselves. Let themselves

git out of it. Git back all of ye," the officer said to the crowd of men and boys now gathering.

A slender woman, slender even in the plaid shawl wrapped over her cloak, lifted her face and took up the prayer. John gasped. It was Frances Willard!

The sweet clear voice rose above the winter wind and silenced the barkeeper and the crowd. John made his way through the snow to kneel beside her. She had turned the appeal to liquor dealers into prayer. The bartender glared and muttered to himself.

". . . O God, in the name of our desolate homes, blasted hopes, ruined lives, for the honor of our community, for our happiness, for the good name of our town, in the name of Jesus Christ sweating out the passion of the cross, for the sake of this soul which will be lost, make this man cleanse himself from his heinous sin. O God, open his ears that we may beg, may implore him. . . .

"O God, pity women! Jesus Christ, help the mothers of sons when their husbands betray them. O God, pity women, help them to end this curse! O, tender Christ, torn in Thine consuming agony, give us of Thy tomorrow and tomorrow, endless tomorrows until this man's heart shall melt. We are here, O dying, deathless Christ. . . ."

The bartender clapped his hands to his head and uttered a howl, "Stop it! Stop it! You can have the place, but I won't have you praying my soul into hell!"

But she did not stop, not until whiskey and beer ran like rain over the pavement and into the gutter where she knelt.[2]

The Great War

When the Austrian Archduke Francis Ferdinand's assassination ignited World War I in the summer of 1914, it took most Americans by surprise. By the turn of the nineteenth century, many believed strongly that progress and reason, aided by technology, would triumph over the archaic problem-solving method of war. Indeed, the twentieth century was to be the "Christian Century."

Rather than becoming better, however, mankind had devised new ways to engage in barbaric cruelty, as evidenced by the Great War, as it was initially called. Industrialization had changed battle techniques as whole nations mobilized their resources and hurled them at each other. Machine guns made old-style frontal attacks suicidal. Soldiers dug trenches for their protection against the modern weapons, but poison gas seeped its monstrous way into those furrows. World War I was not one of movement and attack, but a war of attrition. Man became the slave, not the master, of the weapons he had created: poison gas, aerial warfare, tanks, submarines, machine guns.

By 1915 Russia had buried 2.5 million soldiers and twenty percent of its civilians. Six thousand Europeans died for every day of the war, and material losses soared astronomically. After the communist takeover of Russia in 1917, the U.S. entered the conflict. As President Woodrow Wilson explained, "The world must be safe for democracy." Nearly 3 million Americans served, 115,000 of them losing their lives. The following stories came out of America's involvement in the "Great War."

Salvation's Army

Floyd Horton, who was 102 years old in 1995, served briefly in the trenches during World War I. The Illinois veteran ate potato peelings at the battlefront and there suffered a wound that left one arm virtually useless for the rest of his life.

At twenty-six Horton went to Camp Gordon, Georgia for training. On the train ride to the site, an officer put him in charge of one car and gave him a loaded rifle. He had orders to shoot anybody trying to desert.

Following basic training, Horton and his company sailed to France and quickly made their way to the front. He recalled seeing the most forsaken countryside he ever could have imagined.

* * *

Immediately upon arriving at Verdun, the infamous battlefield, Horton and his companions encountered extremely heavy fighting. They dropped to the ground for cover, unable to raise their heads even an inch or they'd run the risk of getting picked off like turkeys. In that fighting a German bullet found its way into Horton's arm. Although a medic gave him initial treatment and said he'd have to leave the front, Horton still had to walk to get to an ambulance, and it was a long hike at that. Then they had to wait for the all-clear to get to the nearest hospital.

Horton endured the lengthy trip in the dark. When they finally reached the hospital, he was amazed to find that the Salvation Army was there, waiting to minister to the wounded. Their coffee and doughnuts, served with love and compassion, made a lifelong impression on the GI.[1]

Theodore Roosevelt's Admonition

Before Theodore Roosevelt turned fifty, he had written almost thirty books, run a Dakota cattle ranch, conducted scientific expeditions on four continents, been a New York State Congressman, Under-Secretary of the Navy, New York City Police Commissioner, United States Civil Service Commissioner, New York Governor, William McKinley's Vice President and President of the United States.

He read at least five books a week, rode horses, hunted big game, boxed, wrestled, taught Sunday school in his Dutch Reformed church and won the Nobel Peace Prize in 1905. He is known for leading the charge up San Juan Hill in the Spanish-American War and his almost boundless physical energy.

As President, "TR" became known for his toothy smile and his pithy saying, "Speak softly and carry a big stick." He ruffled segregationists' feathers by entertaining Booker T. Washington in the White House, and irritated overweight generals by requiring them to take challenging horseback rides.

By the time America entered World War I, Roosevelt had become a private citizen, but the nation still looked to him for advice and wisdom. The New York Bible Society appealed to the former president to write a message in the New Testaments it would give each American soldier heading for the European battlefields. Here is what he wrote:

* * *

The teaching of the New Testament is foreshadowed in Micah's verse, "What more doth the Lord require of thee than to *do justice*, and to *love mercy*, and to *walk humbly* with thy God." *Do justice*; and therefore fight valiantly against those that stand for the reign of Moloch and Beelzebub on this earth. *Love mercy*; treat your enemies well; succor the afflicted; treat every woman as if she were your sister; care for the little children; and be tender with the old and helpless. *Walk humbly*;

you will do so if you study the life and teachings of the Savior, walking in His steps. And remember: the most perfect machinery of government will not keep us as a nation from destruction if there is not within us a soul. No abounding of material prosperity shall avail us if our spiritual senses atrophy. The foes of our own household will surely prevail against us unless there be in our people an inner life which gives its outward expression in a morality like unto that preached by the seers and prophets of God when the grandeur that was Greece and the glory that was Rome still lay in the future.[2]

Sergeant York, Hero

The ultimate war hero, Alvin Cullem York, was born in the Tennessee mountains on December 13, 1887. His blacksmithing and farming family included seven other boys and three girls, all sharing a one-room cabin. York's education ended around the third grade, which wasn't unusual in that place and time. There weren't many schools to begin with, and those that did exist only operated up to three months a year. He went during the summers for a few years, if and when tobacco production slowed.

Mr. and Mrs. York taught their third son what was most necessary in life—how to handle a plow, a rifle and a Bible. Nevertheless, Alvin strayed from the fold in his youth. He said:

> . . . in my early days, I got in bad company and I broke off from my mother's and father's advice and got to drinking and gambling and playing up right smart. . . . I had a powerful lot of fist fights. I never was whipped, except when my mother and father whipped me.[3]

When York realized that he was breaking his mother's heart and that he had no chance of winning the heart of his beloved Miss Gracie Williams the way he was, he gave up drinking, swearing, chewing and fighting. Another life change quickly followed. Under the influence of evangelist M.H. Russell, York became a Christian.

York had made his peace with his family, his sweetheart and the Lord, but the world was not at peace. Alvin received a notice to register for the draft in June, 1917 while working on a state highway—one that, ironically, would come to be named for him. Although he reported to his local board, the twenty-nine-year-old struggled and prayed over the idea of killing men in a war. As a Christian, York believed killing was wrong. As a York, he remembered his proud heritage, those honored ancestors who had fought in the Revolution, Civil War and Mexican-American War. He recalled:

> I didn't know what to do. I'm telling you there was a war going on inside me, and I didn't know which side to lean to. I was a heap bothered. It is a most awful thing when the wishes of your God and your country . . . get mixed up and go against each other. One moment I would make up my

mind to follow God, and the next I would hesitate and almost make up my mind to follow Uncle Sam. I wanted to follow both but I couldn't. They were opposite. I wanted to be a good Christian and a good American too.[4]

For two days Alvin York went up on the mountainside to pray. He came to believe that it was all right to fight in this war and, furthermore, that he would return unscathed. York realized that in order to be a man of peace, he first had to help win this war.

Although his pastor tried to get him excused from armed service based on conscientious objection, York refused to sign the papers. He later recalled, "I never asked for exemption from service on any grounds at all. I never was a conscientious objector. I am not today. I didn't want to go and fight and kill. But I had to answer the call of my country, and I did."[5]

In the winter of 1917-18 York was sent to Company G, 328th Infantry, 82nd Division armed with his weapons of war and a New Testament that he read five times through while serving his country. "It was my rock to cling to," he said.

In the fall of 1918, only weeks before the war ended, then-corporal York found himself in France's Argonne Forest, one of the war's deadliest arenas. On a particularly awful day, he watched men fall all around him while trying to evade bullets and poison gas. He looked up to the heavens and cried,

O Jesus, the great rock of foundation,
Whereon my feet were set with sovereign
     grace;

Through shells or death with all their
    agitation
Thou wilt protect me if I will only trust in
    Thy grace.
Bless Thy Holy Name!

In that forest the Lord heard the desperate prayer of a simple mountain man. His response made York's name a household word. Although the world showered honors upon him for his bravery, including the Distinguished Service Cross and the French Croix de Guerre, although the New York Stock Exchange ceased trading to venerate him, Alvin York knew full well that the real hero of the Argonne was God.

*   *   *

On October 7, 1918 rain and deadly German shells fell upon Corporal York and his battalion in the forest. The enemy's machine guns were too far away to be used against them, but airplanes buzzed overhead like hornets. Artillery fire killed and wounded dozens of York's compatriots. The woods looked like a tornado had torn through them, reminding the strapping redhead of Revelation's "abomination of desolation." His simple, quiet cabin in Tennessee's Wolf Valley seemed far away indeed.

Orders came during the night for his company to take Hill 223. "Zero hour" would come just before daylight, at 6 o'clock. The men were told to go over the top of Chattel Chehery hill, seize control of it, then advance across the valley to the ridges on the other side. Their objective—the strategically important Decauville Railroad.

At 6:10 the Americans went over the hill and advanced toward the valley. Suddenly the Germans turned their machine guns on them from three directions. "I could see my pals getting picked off until it almost looked like there was none left," wrote York in his diary. "Our losses were very heavy."

Hundreds died within minutes. The Germans soon outnumbered them ten to one. "Our boys just went down like the long grass before the mowing machine at home," he said.

Finding himself with no artillery support and the attack fading, York knew that the machine gun nest had to be taken out. He and the remaining men quickly decided that their best chance was a surprise attack on the Germans (who were hidden on the ridges to their front and left) from the rear.

"According to orders, we advanced through our front line and on through the brush and up the hill on the left. We went very quietly and quickly," York said. "Without any loss and in right smart time, we were across the valley and on the hill where the machine guns were emplaced. The brush and the hilly nature of the country hid us from the Germans."

He and his men were now about 300 yards in front of their own front line. Some of them wanted to attack from the flank, but York, Corporal Early and some others decided to go up over the hill and attack the Germans from the rear.

York said, "We opened up in skirmishing order and flitting from brush to brush, quickly crossed over the hill and down into the gully behind. Then we suddenly swung around behind them."

At that point, they saw a few Germans with Red Crosses on their armbands. York called them to surrender, fearing they would give the Americans away. As the chase ensued, York and the others jumped across a small stream and there encountered up to 20 Germans at their breakfast. Only the major was armed. They threw up their hands in surrender and hollered, "Kamerad!"

"I guess they thought the whole American army was in their rear," York said. "And we didn't stop to tell them anything different."

Now some Germans up on the hill started shooting at them, killing six and wounding another three. With just eight men left in his unit, York became the ranking officer. He recalled the bitter scene, with machine guns "spitting fire and cutting down the undergrowth all around me something awful. You never heard such a racket in all of your life. I didn't have time to dodge behind a tree or dive into the brush. I didn't even have time to kneel or lie down."

The other seven men were too busy guarding their German prisoners to get off any shots. But York did. He put his mountain training to good use as he started firing against roughly thirty machine guns. "In order to sight me or to swing their machine guns on me, the Germans had to show their heads above the trench," he said, "and every time I saw a head I just touched it off. All the time I kept yelling at them to come down. I didn't want to kill any more than I had to."

Just then six Germans jumped out of the trench and charged York with fixed bayonets. An officer fired at him from behind. York said he "changed to the old automatic and just touched them off too. I touched off the sixth man first, then the fifth, then the fourth, then the third and so on. I wanted them to keep coming. I didn't want the rear ones to see me touching off the front ones. I was afraid they would drop down and pump a volley into me."

Finally the German major yelled that if York stopped shooting, the machine gunners would too. When he agreed, the officer blew a whistle, and the men surrendered.

York had killed over twenty men by that time. As the Germans gave up, he covered their commander with his automatic and said he would kill him if the men in the trenches kept shooting. The German gave the signal, and those men also ceased firing. All but one, that is. Right before he reached York, he tossed a small hand grenade that burst in front of the American. "I had to touch him off," York said. "The rest surrendered without any more trouble."

"How many do you have there?" one of York's astonished men asked. "I got a-plenty," he answered.

As it turned out, the German major spoke English "as well as I could," said York. The officer kept his hands up while ordering his men into a column of twos. York assigned his remaining men to both sides of the column while one guarded the rear. Then he ordered the prisoners to pick up and carry the wounded Americans.

"I took the major and placed him at the head of the column," York said, "and I got behind him and used him as a screen. I poked the automatic in his back and told him to hike. And he hiked." York recalled:

It was their second line that I had captured. We sure did get a long way behind the German trenches! And so I marched them straight at that old German front line trench. And some more machine guns swung around and began to spit at us. I told the major to blow his whistle or I would take off his head and theirs too. So he blew his whistle and they all surrendered—all except one. I made the major order him to surrender twice. But he wouldn't. And I had to touch him off. I hated to do it. But I couldn't afford to take any chances and so I had to let him have it.

By that time York had captured well over 100 prisoners. He was deeply concerned about getting them safely to the American lines. "There were so many of them," he said, "there was danger of our own artillery mistaking us for a German counterattack and opening up on us."

At last, York ran into the relief squads sent to help his company. He took the POWs to the battalion post of command. Lieutenant Woods of the Intelligence Department asked in amazement, "York, have you captured the whole German army?" The quiet corporal answered, "A tolerable few."

York was ordered to take the prisoners to regimental headquarters at Chattel Chehery and from there back to division HQ. There they would be turned over to the military police. The group faced constant shell fire, so York hurried them along to get them to safety. "There was nothing to be gained by having any more of them wounded or killed. They had surrendered to me, and it was up to me to look after them. And so I did," he said.

When York reported to Brigadier General Lindsey, he said, "Well, York, I hear you have captured the whole German army." "No, sir," York responded. "I only got 132."

Reflecting on his amazing experience, Alvin York said:

So you can see here in this case of mine where God helped me out. I had been living for God and working in the church some time before I come to the army. So I am a witness to the fact that God did help me out of that hard battle; for the bushes were shot up all around me and I never got a scratch.

So you can see that God will be with you if you will only trust Him; and I say that He did save me. Now, He will save you if you will only trust Him.

York biographer John Perry has said:

He is a hero because he had the moral foundation to be a hero. Certainly he had his faults and shortcomings; even heroes are fallen creatures. But his life was guided by unshakable absolutes founded on the teachings of the Bible, which taught him what was right, and taught him his responsibility in seeing that right was done, regardless of the sacrifice.[6]

Clarence Darrow's Dilemma

One of America's most famous criminal lawyers, Clarence Darrow, caused tremendous damage to evangelical Christianity in the 1920s. He represented Tennessee school teacher John Scopes who, prodded by the American Civil Liberties Union, violated a 1925 statute forbidding the teaching of evolution in the classroom. Scopes was arrested, and press from around the country poured into tiny Dayton, Tennessee for the "Monkey Trial." Defending the prosecution, orator William Jennings Bryan allowed himself to be put on the defensive when Darrow began a barrage of questions beginning with, "Do you think the world was made in six days?"

"Not six days of twenty-four hours," Bryan replied. Indeed, he said after more provoking questions, the world might have been made over a course of millions of years. The presiding judge stopped the inquisition, but Bryan insisted that he believed in the "Rock of Ages, not the ages of rocks."

Though Darrow lost the case (Scopes had to pay a token fine), he succeeded in making Bryan look ridiculous, and he won the hearts and minds of the public. Skeptic H.L. Mencken, who covered the trial in person, predicted the death of fundamentalism.

Today a large number of secular historians still belittle Bryan (who died in his sleep a few days after the trial ended), as well as his fundamentalist position. Some of his critics were not above using such propagandistic techniques as guilt by association, as evidenced by these comments in one textbook:

The repression of foreigners and foreign ideologies and habits soon carried over to the repression of thought and speech. Here, as among the Klansmen and the "drys," Protestant fundamentalists, demanding an absolutely literal reading of the Bible and resisting all modifications of theology in the light of modern science and biblical criticism, led the assault. . . . Those who cared deeply about American traditions of freedom of expression and personal liberty were most discouraged by the right-wing hysteria, ethnic intolerance, and anti-intellectualism of "normalcy."[1]

Bruised and publicly humiliated, many Christians who believed in the Bible's literal interpretation became defensive about their creationist stance, a position that lasted for decades.

But though Clarence Darrow won in the court of public opinion, he had gained the whole world at the cost of his own soul.

*   *   *

The story is told of Dr. John Herman, whose life's ambition was to meet Clarence Darrow. Both men were in their twilight years when they sat down together. "Now that you've come this far in life and you're not doing much lecturing or writing any more," Herman said, "how would you sum up your life?"

Darrow immediately walked over to a coffee table and picked up a Bible. This surprised Dr. Herman. After all, the lawyer had spent most of his life publicly ridiculing the book he now held.

"This verse in the Bible describes my life," Darrow said, opening to Luke 5:5. Changing the "we" to "I," he read aloud, "I have toiled all the night and have taken nothing."

He replaced the Bible and caught Dr. Herman's eye. "I have lived a life without purpose, without meaning, without direction. I don't know where I came from. And I don't know what I'm doing here. And worst of all, I don't know what's going to happen to me when I punch out of here."[2]

World War II

Following the Great War's end in November 1918, a series of treaties, along with the newly formed League of Nations, gave many world leaders hope for a more peaceful era. Unfortunately some countries craved empire more than harmony. A chain reaction of aggression led to the outbreak of World War II in 1939: Japan violated treaties to build a Pacific kingdom that would be economically independent from the West; the Italian dictator Mussolini invaded Ethiopia, once part of his country's realm; and the fascist Francisco Franco led a revolt against the monarchy in Spain.

Frightened by a repeat of the Great War's horrors, Britain and France appeased Adolph Hitler, who, through force and intimidation, was trying to win back territories Germany had lost in World War I. England's Prime Minister Neville Chamberlain signed the Munich Agreement with Hitler in 1938, the latter promising that he would not completely take over Czechoslovakia, just the "Sudetenland" that he claimed rightfully belonged to Germany. But while

Chamberlain returned to England proclaiming, "I believe it is peace in our time," Hitler was retorting, "If ever that silly old man comes interfering here again with his umbrella, I'll kick him downstairs and jump on his stomach in front of photographers."[1]

Winston Churchill called Chamberlain a fool, and Chamberlain's cabinet accused Churchill of warmongering. On September 1, 1939, when Hitler launched a surprise invasion of Poland, Chamberlain was thoroughly discredited. Two days later England declared war on Germany. From 1939 until the end of 1941, the conflict remained within the European family of nations. When the Japanese launched a surprise attack against the U.S. Pacific Fleet at Pearl Harbor, Hawaii on December 7, 1941, the war went global.

World War II lasted until the spring and summer of 1945. On April 28 Benito Mussolini was shot trying to escape to Switzerland. On the 30th, Hitler committed suicide as the Allied forces seized Berlin from his heinous control. President Franklin D. Roosevelt did not live to see those events or to learn of the victory in Europe on May 8. He had died of a cerebral hemorrhage on April 12, and Harry S Truman became the new U.S. President. It was he who brought the Pacific war to a close in August when the Americans dropped atomic bombs on Hiroshima (August 6) and Nagasaki (August 9). Japan finally agreed to an unconditional surrender on September 2, 1945.

Forty-five million people perished in the Second World War, including 20 million Russians, 4.2 million Germans, 2.2 million Chinese, 1.4 million Japanese, and 405,000 Americans. In addition, 6 million Jews and 3 million other "undesireables" expired in Hitler's death camps. To paraphrase U.S. General Omar Bradley, human beings had become technological giants, but ethical midgets.

Throughout the horrors of the war, Americans turned to the faith of their fathers and mothers, holding to a certain belief that evil cannot go unchecked or ultimately triumph in God's world.

Their Finest Hour

B y late summer 1941 the world's future looked bleak and uncertain as the forces of good and evil clashed like comic book characters, with evil being led by a goose-stepping tyrant and his henchmen.

And evil appeared to be winning; Europe lay crushed under the German fist like an empty tin can. In just ten days Germany's blitzkrieg technique— "lightning war"—had conquered Poland. Within seven weeks Hitler's war machine had overwhelmed Denmark, Norway, Belgium, Luxembourg and France.

Britain, led by that twentieth-century lionheart Winston Churchill, clung to the wings of the Royal Air Force and prayers that God would deliver England from this terrible peril. The great, growly Churchill had appealed to his American counterpart, Franklin Delano Roosevelt, for assistance in the fall of 1940. Although the American president knew his people wanted to maintain neutrality in the European conflict, FDR also

realized they didn't want Britain to succumb to Hitler's death blows. In the winter of 1940-41 Roosevelt suggested a Lend-Lease program of arms and supplies for Britain. As he told Congress:

Suppose that your neighbor's house were on fire, and suppose that you had a length of garden hose which would help put out the fire. You wouldn't charge him for it. You would lend it to him in the expectation that he would return it after the fire was out or replace it if it were damaged.[2]

The Lend-Lease program proved invaluable in England's scrappy fight against Hitler, yet as Churchill sailed to his first meeting with the U.S. president in early August 1941, he knew that ultimately deliverance had to come from a much higher Authority than the United States.

* * *

When Churchill's battleship, the *Prince of Wales*, arrived at Placentia Bay, Newfoundland in war camouflage, it progressed slowly past the more peacefully attired American vessels. Just as Churchill's ship passed Roosevelt's vessel, the *Augusta*, the Americans played "The Star-Spangled Banner," and Churchill, dressed in his blue naval uniform, saluted respectfully. Franklin Roosevelt, wearing a suit and supported by his son, returned the gesture. Then came even dearer music to Churchill's ears: "God Save the King." Moments later

FDR received the Prime Minister aboard the *Augusta* with a hearty shaking of hands.

"At long last, Mr. President," said the great Briton.

"Glad to see you aboard, Mr. Churchill," FDR responded.

The Prime Minister gallantly produced from his pocket a letter from King George, bowing while presenting it to Roosevelt. This concluded, he relaxed a bit, lit a cigar and went below with the President.[3]

On the following day, Sunday, Roosevelt cautiously boarded the *Prince of Wales*. There the two world leaders worshiped together flanked by dozens of their troops. Before them on the ship's quarterdeck stood a simple pulpit draped with the flags of both nations. Two of the world's most powerful leaders, men used to giving—not taking—orders, sat humbly while chaplains, whose names history books do not record, led them to bow humbly before the Almighty.

One of the chaplains read from Joshua 1:5-6: "There shall not any man be able to stand before thee all the days of thy life: as I was with Moses, so will I be with thee: I will not fail thee, nor forsake thee. Be strong and of good courage."

Three hymns were sung that day, each leader choosing personally meaningful ones. Roosevelt requested "For Those in Peril on the Sea," Churchill, "Onward, Christian Soldiers" and "O God, Our Help in Ages Past." Two of the most powerful men on earth, used to receiving glory, now gave it to God alone, seeing themselves as His chosen servants raised up "for such a time as this" (Esther 4:14).

The service deeply moved Churchill, and he described what it was like to his people back home. He spoke of

familiar hymns learned in youth that followed him
through adulthood, reminding him of the timeless, un-
changeable God who would help his people in their present danger. "Onward, Christian Soldiers" challenged
Churchill to think of his countryman as fighting for a noble and righteous cause.

He concluded:

> When I looked upon that densely packed con-
> gregation of fighting men of the same language,
> of the same faith, of the same fundamental laws,
> of the same ideals, and now to a large extent of
> the same interests, and certainly, in different de-
> grees, facing the same danger, it swept across
> me that here was the only hope, but also the
> sure hope, of saving the world from measureless
> degradation.[4]

As a result of Roosevelt and Churchill's meeting,
they issued an eight-point joint declaration of war
aims called the Atlantic Charter "designed to counter
Nazi ideology."[5] But their meeting went further than
a joint statement. Its power lay in the Throne of
heaven at whose feet the leaders of the free world
brought their tributes on board that battleship.

A few days after that worship service, U.S. Supreme
Court Justice Felix Frankfurter shared his impression of
it in a letter to President Roosevelt. While acknow-
ledging the importance of the Atlantic Charter, Frankfurter pointed to their worship of God as even greater:

> We live by symbols and we can't too often re-
> call them. And you two in that ocean . . . in the

setting of that Sunday service, gave meaning to the conflict between civilization and arrogant, brute challenge, and gave promise more powerful and binding than any formal treaty could that civilization has brains and resources that tyranny will not be able to overcome.[6]

D-Day, the Sixth of June

In November 1943 the German war machine was faltering, and Hitler issued a directive telling his army what to do when the Allies invaded Western Europe, certain this would take place the following spring or summer. He sent General Erwin Rommel to instill discipline within the ranks serving in the western theater, as well as to lay mines, barbed wire and other obstacles on the French beaches.

The Allies, who were indeed planning an invasion, had decided to land at Normandy along France's southern beaches, but they kept Hitler guessing about the location right up until D-Day itself. The German leader believed the assault would occur north at the Pas de Calais, at the narrowest spot between England and France in the English Channel.

Under the command of U.S. General Dwight D. Eisenhower, the Allied forces of the United States, Britain and Canada stormed the Norman beaches early on the morning of June 6, 1944, many of them keenly aware of their dependence on God in that terrible situation. On that day alone, nearly 5,000 Americans died.

* * *

General Dwight D. Eisenhower, supreme commander of the Allied forces, visited some of his soldiers the night before D-Day, asking them what their jobs were and where in the States they came from. Eisenhower dreaded what lay ahead for those men, many who would never see their loved ones or homes again, who would die on hostile soil in a foreign land. One paratrooper, seeing the general frown, assured him, "Now quit worrying, General, we'll take care of this thing for you."[7]

In his invasion field order to all the troops, the general didn't mince words about what they would face. Nor did he hesitate to share the one thing he knew would give them courage and success: "Your enemy is well trained, well equipped and battle-hardened. He will fight savagely. . . . [Therefore] beseech the blessings of Almighty God on this great and noble undertaking."[8]

The great general was not alone in his sentiments. Recognizing the severity of the situation, one colonel in the 101st Airborne Division told his battalion the night before D-Day, "Men, get on your knees. Now I'm not a religious man, but I want you to get on your knees." Then he prayed briefly for his men.[9] That colonel died in the "first wave."

Back home President Roosevelt led the nation in prayer:

Almighty God: Our sons, pride of our nation, this day have set upon a mighty endeavor, a struggle to preserve our Republic, our religion and our civilization, and to set free a suffering humanity. Lead them straight and true; give strength to their arms, stoutness to their hearts, steadfastness in their faith. They will need Thy blessings.

Their road will be long and hard. For the enemy is strong. He may hurl back our forces. They will be sore tried, by night and by day. . . . The darkness will be rent by noise and flame. Men's souls will be shaken with the violences of war. . . . Success may not come with rushing speed, but we shall return again and again; and we know by Thy grace, and by the righteousness of our cause, our sons will triumph.

Some will never return. Embrace these, Father, and receive them, Thy heroic servants, into Thy kingdom.

And for us at home—fathers, mothers, children, wives, sisters and brothers of brave men overseas, whose thoughts and prayers are ever with them—help us, Almighty God, to rededicate ourselves in renewed faith in Thee in this hour of great sacrifice. . . .

With Thy blessing, we shall prevail over the unholy forces of our enemy. Help us to conquer the apostles of greed and racial arrogance. Lead us to the saving of our country, and with our sister nations into a world unity that will spell a sure peace—a peace invulnerable to the schemings of unworthy men. And a peace that will let all men live in freedom, reaping the just rewards of their honest toil.[10]

In the United States stores closed and baseball games were cancelled. At a Brooklyn shipyard husky welders knelt on the decks and said the Lord's Prayer together. At the opening of the New York Stock Exchange traders observed two minutes of silent prayer. Church bells pealed across America, while the venerable Liberty Bell tolled in Philadelphia. At 7:30 that night traffic stopped in Columbus, Ohio as people prayed in the streets for five minutes.[11]

Back in England priests sent the men off from their embarkation points with the sign of the cross while others held services on the piers. One paratrooper, sitting in his plane with his rosary, was overheard making a vow that he'd never violate the sixth commandment again. A buddy prayed, "Lord, please don't let me get anybody killed and don't let me get killed either. I really think I'm too young for this." Yet another prayed repeatedly, "Give me guts."[12] Each in his own way tried to make peace with God, knowing he might be meeting Him very soon.

They would all need "guts" that morning, traversing across seas so churned up that the Germans were initially surprised by the waves of soldiers who stormed the beaches. Who would chance such a thing in those conditions? But the Allied troops were so determined that after retching all over each other on their landing vessels, they waded determinedly on wobbly legs into the water, careful to keep their weapons dry as they encountered German machine gun fire.

The Utah Beach landing went better than expected. Not so for Omaha where men lay on the beach paralyzed by fear while the Germans rained down their firepower on the Allies. "In 10 minutes one rifle company of 205 men had 197 of them killed or wounded, including every officer and sergeant. With ruined radios, soldiers ashore couldn't tell the ships to stop the further waves from landing and crowding onto [the sand]." After several hours, "one officer, sick of the carnage, stood up and shouted, 'Two kinds of people are staying on this beach, the dead and those who are going to die.' That did it. The deadlock was broken, and in the next 24 hours 175,000 men and 50,000 vehicles came ashore."[13]

Ultimately the invasion so wore down and confused the German forces that it marked the beginning of the Nazi end. The Allies essentially won World War II at D-Day, although the retreating Germans would continue fighting for another year. God had answered millions of prayers for that righteous cause.

Einstein's Humble Present

The twentieth century's most famous scientist, Albert Einstein, was also one of its most-loved figures. Born in Germany in 1879, Einstein had a contradictory and rather unpromising start in life. Although he didn't talk until he reached three, the precocious boy taught himself Euclidean geometry at twelve. He intensely hated dull, rote educational systems and at the Swiss National Polytechnic, Einstein frequently cut classes to study physics solo or play his violin. Not surprisingly, his professors turned him down for a teaching position. Instead Einstein worked as a tutor, substitute teacher and an examiner in the Swiss patent office.

In 1905 his dissertation on the dimensions of molecules secured him a doctorate from the University of Zurich. That year he also published three theoretical papers that eventually changed the way scientists regarded light and motion.

Like Sir Isaac Newton, Einstein believed in a universe ordered by God. While adherents of the quantum theory of the fundamental character of matter rejected his notion of strict causality, Einstein insisted, "God does not play dice [with the universe]."[1]

As a Jew, Einstein was passionately involved in the causes of pacifism (he criticized the German aggression that led to World War I) and Zionism (the right of Jews to return to their homeland in Israel) and became a target of malicious anti-Semitic attacks. When Adolph Hitler came to power in 1933, Einstein accepted a position at Princeton, New Jersey's Institute for Advanced Study, where his name became synonymous with the town.

During his life in Princeton, Einstein became a beloved and familiar figure who was frequently seen taking walks and examining the kitchen gadgets at Woolworth's on Nassau Street. Sometimes visitors to Princeton mistook him for a bum because of his unkempt appearance and finger-in-the-light-socket hair. Always approachable, the kindly professor, whose theories rocked the scientific community, helped a little neighbor who was struggling with his math homework. One night his gentleness touched a group of Princeton Seminarians.

*   *   *

On a cold December night just before Christmas 1947, Princeton Seminary student David Crawford and eight of his friends went caroling in the venerable neighborhood around the campus. As they advanced up Mercer Street toward the seminary, the group paused before the legendary professor's house.

"Of course we won't go see the Einsteins," one of the students said.

"Well, why not?" asked Crawford.

"It's Christmas. What will we sing?"

Everyone knew the professor was Jewish, but Crawford and the others persisted because, after all, Dr. Einstein frequently attended services at Miller Chapel. They had often laughed quietly as Princeton Seminary President John Alexander Mackay would say at the close of worship, "We will wait here until Professor Einstein passes out."

"Maybe we should sing 'Jingle Bells,' " one of the fellows suggested as he stamped his feet on the cold, clear sidewalk.

"That's ecumenical," another agreed, nodding.

"I think we should sing 'Silent Night' in German," someone else said. "That would be nice."

The fellows reluctantly agreed and moved up the steps to ring the doorbell. When Professor Einstein appeared smiling, the young seminarians started singing the tune in German—badly.

With a twinkle in his eyes he invited the young men into his parlor and offered them candy from a bonbon dish. Then he held up his finger as if to say, "I have something to give to you." Opening the door to the hall closet, Professor Einstein got out his violin and gave the students his own gift—"O Holy Night."

Harry Truman and the Founding of Modern Israel

I n May 1948 Israel became an independent state after wandering throughout the world since Rome destroyed Jerusalem in A.D. 70. A persecuted group through the centuries, the Jews had just suffered the most unspeakable loss of all—Hitler's slaughter of 6 million men, women and children. Their need to return to their homeland was more urgent than ever.

Although the founding of modern Israel occurred on the other side of the world from the United States, an American president played an instrumental role in it. In fact, the story reads a bit like that of Queen Esther, whom God raised up to save the Jews from Haman's plot to annihilate them. At first she acted reluctantly, but was finally persuaded by her uncle Mordecai that God had raised her up "for such a time as this."

* * *

Harry S Truman (the "S" doesn't stand for anything) took the oath of office on April 12 following the death of Franklin Delano Roosevelt. A little over a week later, on the morning of the 20th, Rabbi Stephen S. Wise visited President Truman in the Oval Office. As Chairman of the American Zionist Emergency Council, Wise was particularly eager to secure Truman's support for a Jewish state.

The new President looked forward to the meeting. He had been interested in the land of Palestine/Israel since his youth, partly because of its connection to the Bible and partly because it had always provided a dynamic backdrop to human history.

Rabbi Wise began their discussion by pointing out the dire necessity for a Jewish homeland as World War II drew to its dramatic close. Truman said, "I knew the things that had happened to the Jews in Germany," although he didn't—as he would realize later—know the whole tragic story. That day he pledged to Wise that America would do everything in its power to turn Israel's dream of statehood into reality.

The rabbi politely pointed out that President Truman might meet with resistance from many people in the government, particularly the State Department's Middle East experts. Truman explained that he already had heard from them and had told those "striped-pants boys" in no uncertain terms that while he was President he, and not they, would be making foreign policy.

"Their job," he said, "was to carry it out, and if there were some who didn't like it, they could resign anytime they felt like it."

Three years later, Israel's goal of statehood was still not accomplished. The formation of a Jewish homeland was put in the hands of the newly formed United Nations. Truman announced his belief that the UN would provide a satisfactory solution. To his dismay, however, the President found himself pressured on all sides by American Zionists. They wanted him to do more than just express confidence that the UN would do the right thing. Harry Truman said the outcry was greater than when he had fired General MacArthur. He finally made it known that he wasn't going to receive any "extremists" for the Zionist cause, no matter who they were, because he had "other matters awaiting."

The President didn't count on the American Zionists using his old friend and business partner, Eddie Jacobson, to get through to him, however. One day Jacobson visited Truman in the White House. The President laid the ground rules for their discussion. He said, "Eddie, I'm always glad to see old friends, but there's one thing you've got to promise me. I don't want you to say a word about what's going on over there in the Middle East." Jacobson promised that he wouldn't say a thing.

As they talked about this and that, Truman discovered to his chagrin that Eddie Jacobson was crying. "You promised me you wouldn't say a word about what's going on over there," he reminded his friend.

The truth was, Jacobson hadn't said a word. It was just that "every time I think of the homeless Jews," he said, "homeless for thousands of years . . . I start crying." Jacobson also mentioned that his tears were for Chaim Weizmann, who had spent his entire life working for a Jewish homeland, and who now was an old, sick man. Weizmann was in New York and asking to see Truman.

The President put the brakes on this conversation. They went on to other subjects, but every now and then a great tear rolled down Jacobson's face. Truman said he should have his old friend tossed right out of the Oval Office. "You knew [blank] good and well I couldn't stand seeing you cry," the President said. Jacobson smiled a little and thanked him, then left.

Truman picked up the phone and called the State Department, informing them that he was going to receive Chaim Weizmann. They "carried on" just as he expected, but the President went through with the visit just the same. On May 14 the United States officially recognized Israel's statehood eleven minutes after it was announced.

A year later Israel's chief rabbi visited President Truman at the White House. Like a prophet of old he told the Chief Executive, "God put you in your mother's womb so that you could be the instrument to bring about the rebirth of Israel after two thousand years."

Truman, like his friend Eddie Jacobson, felt a large tear slide down his cheek.[1]

The Voice of the Century

"T he Voice of the Century" belonged to Philadelphian Marian Anderson. Born in the black section of the city in 1902, she became the first American of African descent to perform with New York's Metropolitan Opera. At the beginning of her singing career, however, Miss Anderson performed mostly for European audiences because the larger American venues prohibited blacks from appearing in them. She did not complain, however, preferring to let her talent make a case for her. She endured many snubs and outrageous limits because of prejudice, but Miss Anderson endured them quietly and with great dignity. One time she received the key to Atlantic City, New Jersey, only to be refused a hotel room there, and when Miss Anderson sang at the premier of a movie about Abraham Lincoln in Illinois, the Lincoln Hotel refused her lodging.

The elegant singer kept such sorry episodes low-key, but the most trying racial incident she ever encountered went very public.

*   *   *

It began in mid-1938 when Howard University in Washington, D.C. invited her to sing. Constitution Hall, owned by the Daughters of the American Revolution (DAR), was the only place in the city large enough to accommodate the expected crowds. But when Miss Anderson's agent, Sol Hurok, tried to make reservations for the April 9, 1939 concert, he was informed that the hall was reserved for that date. Hurok submitted other dates, but all were turned down. Finally he asked another concert master to request the same dates and found out that every one was available. It became obvious that Negroes were not welcome at Constitution Hall.

Shock waves pulsed through the music world, and several well-known artists cancelled their appearances at the Hall. Violinist Jascha Heifetz remarked, "I am ashamed to play at Constitution Hall." First Lady Eleanor Roosevelt publicly revoked her membership from the DAR in her newspaper column, "My Day," creating a major sensation. Other prominent women quit the DAR as well, and several local chapters lodged protests.

The United States Department of the Interior offered to let Miss Anderson sing at an outdoor concert at the Lincoln Memorial on Easter Sunday. She reluctantly agreed. The affair had upset her, but like it or not, said Hurok, she had become a symbol of her race. She appeared that day, nervous and determined as Secretary of the Interior Harold Ickes introduced her to the audience of 75,000.

Her voice rose like a benediction over her enraptured

listeners in song after song. When the concert ended, the crisp spring air reverberated with stormy applause. Miss Anderson stepped to the microphone saying, "I am overwhelmed. I can't tell you what you have done for me today. I thank you from the bottom of my heart again and again." Kosti Vehanen (her accompanist) remarked, "God in His great wisdom opened the door to His most beautiful cathedral . . . that glorious Easter Sunday."

Four years later in 1943 Secretary Ickes unveiled a mural of the event at the Department of the Interior. He said, "Marian Anderson's voice and personality have come to be a symbol of the willing acceptance of the immortal truth that 'all men are created equal.'" The following day she sang at Constitution Hall at the request of the DAR at a war benefit for China Relief.[1]

A Decision for Life

On January 22, 1973 the United States Supreme Court ruled that women have a guaranteed right to an abortion during a pregnancy's first trimester. It also permitted the government to regulate second-trimester abortions in the interest of the mother's health. This was the infamous Roe v. Wade decision, brought by Norma McCorvey under her alias, Jane Roe, against Henry B. Wade, a Texas district attorney, in 1969. Since that ruling, tens of millions of unborn children have perished.

This court decision was particularly significant for Joe Terry, a member of the popular 1950s band "Danny and the Juniors," and his wife, Joyce. During those impassioned years of debate about abortion, they faced a true "crisis pregnancy." A rare blood disease led to the doctors' grim prediction that unless Joyce got an abortion, she probably would not live, nor would her baby. At a low ebb in his singing career and in his life in general, Joe thought an abortion might be the right answer—until Someone convinced him otherwise. The following is Joe's story, in his own words.

*   *   *

The rain pelted against my windshield, driving a deep chill through my anxious spirit as I drove to the drug store. My wife and I had left our two children with her mother so we could come to the Catskills looking for answers to our problems. So far all we got were terrible colds. Joyce sat beside me in the passenger seat, too sick and discouraged for words. That was okay with me. I had nothing to say. Everything was a mess. My career had hit a dead-end, and I was afraid Joyce was going to die; she was pregnant against the doctors' orders. I didn't know where to turn.

I had got off to such a great start too. When I was 16, I started singing baritone with a group called the Juvenairs. Like many young performers in Philadelphia, we sang on street corners. One night in 1957 we got the attention of record producer John Madara by singing under his window. "Get lost!" he shouted. "You're waking my kids." We persisted, though, and he finally came downstairs in his bathrobe to listen.

In a few dizzying weeks we changed our name to Danny and the Juniors (our lead singer was Danny Rapp) and made a hit appearance on Dick Clark's "American Bandstand." Our song "At the Hop" skyrocketed to the top of the American record charts like an Atlas missile. It orbited there for seven incredible weeks and sold 2.5 million copies of the record. Our next song, "Rock 'n' Roll is Here to Stay," became a teenage anthem.

Altogether Danny and the Juniors made 114 appearances on "American Bandstand" alone. We sang our first two hits plus "Twistin' U.S.A.," "Pony Express," "Dottie" and many other songs to screaming audiences worldwide. It was like something you dream about. For me that time really was like the "Happy Days" TV show. My biggest problem in life was getting homework done. After concerts I'd look for the girls who wore glasses and ask them if they knew anything about math!

The magic lasted only six years, though. Following staggering successes, Danny and the Juniors crashed and burned. In 1962 and 1963 our new releases barely got launched. Then the Beatles invaded America's music kingdom. Suddenly the record companies wanted long hair and electric guitars, not the do-wop, street-corner sound.

We broke up in 1964, and I decided to go solo. One eager promoter told me, "Change your name to Finkle Farkle. You'll be a big success." "Absolutely not!" I told him. "I'll never be Finkle Farkle." But I did become Jude Nova, Jude after "Hey Jude," and Nova because my last name is Terranova. I gave in a little to the trends without selling myself even more. It was still a bust, though. In less than a year, I returned to my former stage name, "Joe Terry." I couldn't seem to do anything right.

I went from "American Bandstand" to a Philadelphia cab stand. I took up taxi driving to keep a roof over my young family's head while I wrote songs on the side, songs nobody wanted to hear. I found it really embarrassing when people would get into the cab and say, "I've seen you before. You're from

Danny and the Juniors." I'd tell them, "No, that's my brother."

I also started drinking—heavily. A lot of performers in my position did. I became hard to live with. When Joyce found out she was pregnant for the third time, the bottom fell out of my life.

The first time Joyce got pregnant, she kept blacking out and constantly felt exhausted. At first the doctors feared she had leukemia. Then they discovered that the problem was thalassemia, an abnormality in the red blood cells. (It's also known as Mediterranean Anemia because many people from that area get it.) The doctors gave Joyce five blood transfusions during her pregnancy, and she ate steak or liver every night for dinner to build up her red blood cells.

Joyce made it through the first time, and we had a healthy son, Joseph, whom we call Terry. The doctors advised us not to have more children. "Every time," they said, "the risks to the mother and child become greater."

We found out how true that was when Joyce got pregnant with our daughter, Vicky. After one blood transfusion, Joyce got hepatitis and nearly died. "Any more children after this," the doctors warned, "and you're courting disaster." Amazingly, my wife got pregnant again. The doctors thought an abortion was the answer.

"You know you'll both probably die otherwise," one of them told her.

Our families sided with the physicians. "Use your head, Joyce," they said. "You have two beautiful children. Do you realize what could happen?"

We did. If Joyce died, our kids would be left with a father who could barely cope with his own life, let alone theirs. The doctors tried to sway us. They suggested probable odds then added, "We hope to God that you don't go through with this."

There was so much to think about. I was doing the cab thing, drinking to excess and failing constantly at jump-starting my career. I wasn't sure what Joyce should do. I didn't like the idea of abortion, but then again, my wife's life was in danger, and I needed her. When I asked her what she wanted to do, Joyce said, "God has been with me my whole life. He'll get me through this."

I couldn't figure out why she wanted this baby so much when we already had two children. Nor did I share her faith. This was 1970 and, like many young people, I was questioning God. Now I needed answers, and fast. I thought that by going to the Catskills, I could get a singing job, and everything would be all right again. Inwardly, though, I knew something more than music was missing from my life.

I did not get the job I so desired. As I drove to the drug store in the pouring rain, I knew that if something didn't give soon, I'd give up. I was standing on the edge of an emotional cliff and knew it wouldn't take much to get me to jump.

I pulled into the parking lot and turned off the car. Steeling myself against the downpour, I hurried into the pharmacy. Right then and there my emotions spilled over like so many rain drops. I silently cried out in anguish to a God I wasn't sure existed. It surprised me. *Maybe it's because I used to believe when I was a kid*, I reasoned.

My parents had sent me to catechism and church when I was growing up, and I had faith then. I also remembered how, right before Danny and the Juniors made it big, sometimes late at night, I'd sit up and watch TV. I don't know why, but I would get this overwhelming feeling of God's goodness. It made me feel good about life too. It was strange and wonderful.

Then the group made it big, and I started ignoring God. Once in a while on the road, though, I'd see a church and go inside. At the same time, though, I explored other religions. It all left me feeling empty and afraid.

The gray-haired pharmacist cleared his throat, interrupting my disturbed thoughts. "May I help you?" he asked. He was a friendly-looking man.

"I have two prescriptions for Terranova," I muttered.

As he shuffled off to get them, I reached into my pocket for my wallet. That's when my eye caught a rack full of thirty-five cent pamphlets on the counter. One of them practically reached out and grabbed me by the heart. It was called, "How to Keep Your Faith." When I read the title, I suddenly *knew* what my problem was—I had lost my faith—in God, in myself, in everything.

The whole terrible mess of my life started making sense as that same peaceful feeling I had known as a teenager overwhelmed me once again with a sense of God's goodness. Fear peeled away like the skin off a ripe orange, leaving me refreshed and at peace for the first time in years.

"I'll take this too," I told the druggist, holding up the booklet. It was God's answer to my desperate prayer for help. I knew that the simple message would go further to heal me than any prescription. I skipped out to the car like Gene Kelly in "Singin' in the Rain" and told Joyce what had happened. "God's going to work everything out," I said. She was incredulous. Her eyes welled up with tears as she laid her hand on mine. "I have you back again." She smiled weakly. "It was like I had lost you, like you had become some other person."

God began renewing every area of my life. A few months before Joyce's due date, Danny and the Juniors accepted a low-paying gig at the Academy of Music in New York's Greenwich Village. We headlined twelve rock 'n roll acts, and the show was a huge success. The – '50s nostalgia movement, which would result in the movie "American Graffiti" and the TV shows "Happy Days" and "Laverne and Shirley," had started.

A month later we did another triumphant rock 'n roll show, this time at Madison Square Garden. Danny and the Juniors began touring the country as the '50s "revival" broke out first in one part of the U.S., then another.

One thing remained—Joyce's high-risk delivery. When my wife went into labor in January of 1971, I had some anxious moments. While she was in the delivery room, I went to the snack shop for coffee. On the way back upstairs, there was a code blue in maternity. I just knew something was wrong with Joyce. A bunch of doctors crowded into the elevator with me, and I got very upset. "It's my wife," I kept saying. "I know it's my wife." They managed to throw me off, telling me everything would be all right.

I went back to the waiting room to calm down, to draw on the faith reserves I'd just started building up. When I got composed again, leaning on the good God I knew was with us, I got back on the elevator. A nurse was there with a tiny baby. "How cute!" I said.

"Yes, it's the Terranova baby," she answered. "It's a boy."

"That's my son!" I cried out. My cup overflowed.

As it turned out, Joyce was fine, too. The code blue had been an unfortunate mix-up.

With Raymond's birth, I had everything I wanted—a loving, dedicated wife, three healthy children, a thriving singing career and, best of all, my faith in God. My life was a tiny bit like Job's—what came after my afflictions was even better than what had come before.

God brought Raymond into my life when I didn't know how or if I could go on. Today he is a constant reminder that God can fix the most broken problems I have if I just leave them in His hands. While I'm awfully glad that rock 'n' roll is here to stay, it means far more to me that the same can be said for my faith in God.[1]

Man in Space

The space race between the United States and
Russia began in earnest in late 1957 when the
Soviets launched *Sputnik*, the first successful
satellite. In May 1961 newly inaugurated President
John F. Kennedy initiated the *Apollo* program, designed to land a man on the moon and return him
safely by the end of the 1960s.

Flight after flight made deep impressions on people
the world over as science and technology combined to
bring to reality the age-old dream of reaching another
heavenly body. It seemed to many that God and the Bible had become obsolete in the face of such stellar human accomplishments. One only needs to check the
record, however, to realize how much God meant to the
manned spaced program: the men of *Apollo 8* read from
the Bible during their mission. The people of the whole
world lifted up the *Apollo 13* astronauts in prayer, holding their breath as the men struggled to bring their crippled spacecraft back to earth. And astronaut James
Irwin became a dedicated Christian after his *Apollo 15*
moon mission.

In the Beginning . . .

On December 21, 1968 the crew of *Apollo 8* roared into space toward the moon carrying Commander Frank Borman, Jim Lovell and William Anders. A landmark flight, *Apollo 8* circled the moon ten times in twenty hours in preparation for the first lunar landing that would occur the following summer. On Christmas Eve the astronauts, who became the first to reach the moon, transmitted startling images of the earth at roughly 8:40 p.m. (EST). Then they gave the world another deeply moving Christmas present.

* * *

"For all the people on Earth the crew of *Apollo 8* has a message we would like to send you," said William Anders. He turned to the first chapter of the Bible and began to read:

In the beginning God created the heaven and the earth. And the earth was without form, and void; and darkness was upon the face of the deep. And the Spirit of God moved upon the face of the waters. And God said, Let there be light: and there was light. And God saw the light, that it was good: and God divided the light from the darkness. (Genesis 1:1-4)

James Lovell took the Bible and read the next four verses as *Apollo 8* orbited the moon:

> And God called the light Day, and the darkness he called Night. And the evening and the morning were the first day. And God said, let there be a firmament in the midst of the waters, and let it divide the waters from the waters. And God made the firmament, and divided the waters which were under the firmament from the waters which were above the firmament: and it was so. And God called the firmament Heaven. And the evening and the morning were the second day. (1:5-8)

Lovell handed the Bible to Commander Frank Borman, who completed the moving Christmas Eve reading of the Creation account, the one so many scientists had abandoned in favor of Darwin's evolutionary theory:

> And God said, Let the waters under the heaven be gathered together unto one place, and let the dry land appear: and it was so. And God called the dry land Earth; and the gathering together of the waters he called the Seas: and God saw that it was good. And God said, Let the earth bring forth grass, the herb yielding seed, and the fruit tree yielding fruit after his kind, whose seed is in itself, upon the earth; and it was so. And the earth brought forth grass, and herb yielding seed after his kind, and the tree yielding seed after his kind, and the tree yielding fruit, whose seed was

in itself, after his kind: and God saw that it was
good. (1:9-12)

When Borman finished the reading, he closed the
Bible saying, "And from the crew of *Apollo 8*, we close
with good night, good luck, a Merry Christmas, and
God bless all of you—all of you on the good Earth."[1]

Apollo 13

James Lovell of *Apollo 8* left for the moon with
Fred W. Haise, Jr. and John L. Swigert, Jr. on
April 11, 1970. The first two days went so
smoothly that CapCom Joe Kerwin commented,
"The spacecraft is in real good shape as far as we are
concerned. We're bored to tears down here."

Nine hours later, James Lovell and his crew finished
a nearly one-hour television broadcast. The commander closed the program with, "This is the crew of
Apollo 13 wishing everybody there a nice evening, and
we're just about ready to close out our inspection of
Aquarius (the lunar module) and get back for a pleasant evening in *Odyssey* (the command module). Good
night."

Oxygen tank no. 2 blew up nine minutes later: No.
1 followed as the astronauts heard a sharp bang and
felt a strong vibration. Jack Swigert noticed a warning
light and told ground control, "Houston, we've had a
problem here." The light indicated that *Apollo 13*'s
fuel cells were lost, cells that provided most of the

spacecraft's electricity. At 200,000 miles from earth, with their oxygen tanks leaking into space, the situation looked grim.

The astronauts and Houston Ground controllers decided to depend on the lunar module's (LM) systems for survival. According to NASA, "Completely new procedures had to be written and tested in the simulator before being passed up to the crew."[2] The LM was equipped for a forty-five-hour lifetime, not the ninety required to get the crew home alive. Fortunately, it did contain enough oxygen reserves for the men.

The astronauts shut down all non-critical systems and reduced their energy consumption to one-fifth. Physically they had to make adjustments as well, cutting back on their water usage because their space suits had limited storage for body wastes. They ate little—mostly hot dogs and "wet-pack" foods—and became dehydrated. Altogether the three astronauts lost a total of 31.5 pounds, and Fred Haise became seriously ill with a bladder infection. It didn't help him when the temperature in the cabin plummeted to thirty-eight degrees Fahrenheit, with the walls oozing condensation.

The world held its breath, waiting to see whether this would be the first time men would be lost in space or if they would burn up when the space craft reentered the earth's atmosphere. The movie *Apollo 13* showed how the mission control specialists used ingenuity and duct tape to return the astronauts safely. What it left out was the prayers that surely counted for far more.

* * *

The watching world prayed in the tongues of many languages as banner headlines proclaimed the astronauts' plight: "Moon-Shot Life and Death Drama." "Crippled *Apollo* races against time."

At Chicago's Wrigley Field Comedian Milton Berle told the somber spectators, "If I may be serious for one moment—and ask the entire audience for a moment of prayer for the crewmen of the *Apollo 13*. We'll hold silence for a moment, please." He removed his hat as thousands of Cubs fans joined his earnest prayer for the astronauts' safe return.

At the Vatican, Pope Paul VI offered prayers for Lovell, Haise and Swigert while Orthodox Jews in prayer shawls appealed to God on their behalf at Jerusalem's Wailing Wall.

Those prayers and millions more were said on April 17 as the world listened tensely to the astronauts prepare for reentry. As the time neared for them to attempt a splashdown, Commander Lovell thanked everyone at Ground Control, concluding, "You have a good bedside manner." No one listening could help but wonder if those would be among his final words.

As the craft hurled toward earth moments later, it was engulfed by searing flames. The anxious ground control contingent wondered if the heat shield would hold up to the punishing temperatures. The radio blackout lasted a total of three minutes, an excruciatingly slow and tense time. Even if the shield worked, there was great anxiety over where the craft would splash down. If its beacons didn't work, *Apollo 13* could not be visible to its rescuers amidst the vast Pacific Ocean's white caps.

Three minutes came and went, and there was no sign of the spacecraft. Suddenly rescuers pointed and yelled, "There they are! They made it! They made it!"

An ocean of tears splashed down along with the astronauts, as applause reverberated around the world, humanity's "thank-you" to God, who is above and beyond the zenith of human technology and science.

The Asbury College Revival:
God's Student Sit-in

I n 1970, while "the times were a-changin'," college campuses across the United States throbbed with rebellion. The media carried stories daily of students who had discarded their parents' and society's standards in favor of free sex, radical feminism, illegal drugs, eastern religions and acid rock. These were students who also had grown up in prosperity but who rejected materialism and decried the poverty of millions of their countrymen. They denounced environmental damage, consumer waste, racial divisions and the nuclear threat under which they had spent their childhoods. The assassinations of John Kennedy, Martin Luther King, Jr. and Robert Kennedy had left many young people disillusioned about America.

Of all the causes college students took up, however, none was more fervently adopted than protesting the war in Vietnam. Costing tens of thousands of American lives, the conflict's boundaries and rationale were unclear. At many colleges and universities students arranged "sit-in" demonstrations, clogging administration buildings, preventing faculty and staff from reaching their offices and classrooms.

Many of the young radicals helped bring down President Johnson, who didn't attend his own party's convention in Chicago in 1968 because of their fierce and violent rallies against him. When President Nixon announced in the spring of 1970 that he was sending American ground forces into Cambodia to halt the flow of supplies from that country to North Vietnam, students once again set their campuses aflame. Some colleges and universities even closed in protest. Then a tragedy unfolded.

On May 4, 1970 a noontime protest broke out at Ohio's Kent State University. For days students had clashed with local police, breaking windows and inflicting other property damage. Ohio's governor called out the National Guard, but the unit that responded wasn't well-trained in crowd control. When students started stoning the guardsmen, the troops fired into the crowd, killing four students and wounding eleven others. Of those who died, two were female students passing by on their way to class.

Less than two weeks later, police in Mississippi killed two black student protestors at Jackson State University. Americans shook their heads as they watched the anguish on television, wondering what this generation was coming to.

Not all students were protesting, but the most vocal and dramatic ones (who were, in fact, a minority) commanded the most media attention.

During that unsettled time in American history, many other college students were undergoing a different kind of change. The "Jesus Movement" had broken out, with thousands of young people turning on to Jesus, tuning into the Holy Spirit and dropping out of the quest for meaning via sex, drugs and rock 'n' roll. Nowhere was this more visible than at a small Methodist college near Lexington, Kentucky, where God set the campus aflame with His presence that convulsive spring of 1970.

On a cold and windy February day, 1,000 Asburians gathered for 10 a.m. chapel in venerable Hughes Auditorium, seated according to their classes. The dean had been scheduled to preach, but at the last minute he decided to give a testimony about what God was doing in his life. Then he offered to let a few students do the same. Lately on campus there had been a great sense of expectation that God was about to manifest Himself in a mighty way, and many had been praying fervently for revival.

A few students stepped to the platform to tell heartfelt stories of God's grace in their lives. As they spoke, a sense of God's presence filled the auditorium. The chapel period came to an end and one professor called any students who wanted to pray to come forward and kneel at the altar. Unexpectedly, a mass of Asburians thronged toward the front as everyone took up the hymn, "Just As I Am."

The bell rang for classes to begin, but it went unheeded as student after student began publicly to confess his or her sins. Reconciliations occurred between former enemies and strained relationships were healed.

By noon, the chapel service was still going strong. One professor went to the cafeteria for a department meeting only to discover that the place was nearly deserted. He headed over to Hughes to find out why chapel hadn't ended yet.

The college's administration cancelled the rest of the day's classes. Almost all of the 1,550 seats in Hughes were filled as the service lasted into that evening. One student reported losing track of time with no sense of hunger, thirst or other physical needs.

The revival spread across the street to Asbury Seminary the next day during its scheduled chapel service, and many townspeople from Wilmore, the community surrounding Asbury, came to Hughes Auditorium. As the nonstop service continued into the rest of the week, several local pastors urged their flocks to attend the revival rather than their own church services that Sunday.

Finally, on February 10, a full week after the revival began, the Asbury administration resumed classes at the end of that day's chapel period. They would, however, keep Hughes open for prayer, and nightly meetings would be held there. God's campus "sit-in" had lasted 185 hours, and its effects spread far beyond Wilmore to other campuses as far as California, and even to other countries. This happened wherever Asbury students testified to the remarkable revival during the following months. Here are some of their stories.

* * *

One Asbury student told an Oklahoma bank president about the incredible outpouring of God's Spirit at his college campus and how many students had given their lives even more fully to Christ. The executive admitted that he had been a nominal Christian for years, but now he felt a powerful need for God to move in his life as well. Then they knelt in the office as the bank president gave his life completely to the Lord. Afterwards he called his staff together for a prayer meeting, and the Asburian once again told the story of his school's revival.[1]

*　*　*

Many Asbury students formed "witness teams" that traveled throughout America telling people what had happened at their school. One day they stopped at a gas station run by a recently married couple. As the girls talked to the wife, she confessed that she didn't really love her husband, that she had been infatuated with him and nothing more. Now she felt trapped. One student told her that Jesus could give her a true love for her husband if she confessed her sin and gave her life to the Lord. In the meantime, the guys had been witnessing to the husband about Christ, and he prayed to receive the Lord.[2]

*　*　*

An Asbury coed took a bus to Cincinnati, and her seat partner asked why she was reading the Bible. She told him that she loved God's Word, and then she shared His plan of salvation. The man wanted his friend in another seat to hear the girl's testimony, so the men switched seats, and the coed repeated the story. At that point, an elderly man sitting in front of her asked if she would speak up because he hadn't been able to understand every word. In addition, a woman sitting across from the Asburian wanted to hear more too. At that point the coed rose, went to the front of the bus and gave her testimony to everyone. When the bus arrived in Cincinnati, the driver turned around and asked her, "Do you have anything more to say?"

"All I want to say," she told him, "is hallelujah!"[3]

*   *   *

One Asbury student wrote to her newspaper, the Citizen Patriot, in Jackson, Michigan about the revival:

> There is a new kind of demonstration at Asbury during these days of national college sit-ins—not in the administration offices, but in the college and seminary chapels. Students are throwing around a lot of three-, four-, and five-letter words, too. Words like "joy," "love," "pray," and "faith." They plan to turn the world upside-down, not because they're troublemakers, but for the sake of Jesus Christ![4]

*   *   *

One newsman expressed delight that he was being called upon to cover the revival, having grown sick of reporting student riots. "If those kids run out of something to pray for about 2 o'clock in the morning," he said, "ask them to pray for me."[5]

*   *   *

Don Daniels of the *Wheeling News Register* wrote about the revival in his column on February 8, 1970. He opened with the question, "Did you hear about the love-in at Asbury College?" He pointed out how strange it was to think of a "love-in" at a Christian college, with a seminary across the street to boot. He chronicled how the revival got started and pointed out how amazing and encouraging he thought it all was, especially that young people were doing something truly constructive.

"No news in that, is there?" he asked. Then he answered his own question. "Yes, it is news," he said. "Good, gutty news that tells me there remains on the nation's campuses a hard core sense of morality, and that in the final analysis the mark on history will be written by the people who spurn the podium of militant dissent in favor of a quiet place to talk with God. . . ."

He went on to describe himself as a "busted down Catholic, a sometimes dissident Christian who drinks too much and smokes too much and favors mini-skirts on everyone but my wife and my sister." But he concluded, "I'm gonna get on the side where God is."[6]

There She Is, Miss America

When Heather Whitestone was crowned Miss America on September 17, 1994, it was a milestone in the pageant's history. At the age of eighteen months, Heather contracted a fever after her DPT shots and was hospitalized, near death. The medication given to her caused profound hearing loss. In 1994 she became the first disabled Miss America.

Heather won the nation's heart with her earnest optimism and faith in Christ. These she expressed poignantly in her ballet routine to Sandi Patty's "Via Dolorosa" ("way of sorrow"), a song she couldn't even hear. As she describes in her book, *Listening with My Heart*, Heather had known her own "way of sorrow" along the path to the realization of her dream. Through Christ, she won her greatest contest before she became Miss America.

*   *   *

Following the Miss Deaf Alabama pageant, Heather Whitestone returned home feeling particularly empty. At the core of her struggle was one fundamental question: Was she to live as a hearing-impaired person in a hearing world or function mainly within the safer parameters of the non-hearing world? Her mother had raised Heather for the former way of life, but now the teenager wasn't so sure she wanted to walk in it. She had never felt so alone.

"Over and over I prayed, 'God, who am I? Hearing or deaf?' " she said. "I had sunk to the lowest level of my life, and for a while I wasn't sure I wanted to go on living. The future seemed bleak and hopeless, the past nothing but wasted effort."[1]

Out of that experience Heather started to read the Bible more diligently than ever before. One day the story of Thomas, the disciple who doubted Jesus' resurrection, hit home in a powerful way. As she read, "blessed are those who have not seen and yet have believed" (John 20:29, NIV), the young woman realized that no one can see or hear God. Just like her, a hearing-impaired person, everyone else must know God with their hearts, not their senses. The thought that she was just like everyone else and that God loved her lifted Heather's spirit and guided her from darkness to light.

As she continued reading her Bible, "listening" for God's voice, Heather's loneliness dissipated. "Though I still didn't know where I'd find a place in this world," she said, "I knew that I was in capable hands—God's."[2]

Endnotes

Christopher Columbus

[1] Peter Marshall and David Manuel, *The Light and the Glory* (Grand Rapids, MI: Revell, 1977), p. 17.
[2] Ibid., p. 41.

Pocahontas

[1] Robert S. Tilton, *Pocahontas: The Evolution of an American Narrative* (New York: Cambridge University Press, 1994), p. 14.
[2] Ibid., p. xvi.

Pilgrims and Puritans

[1] Marshall and Manuel, p. 148.
[2] Samuel Eliot Morison, Henry Steele Commager and William E. Leuchtenburg, *The Growth of the American Republic* (New York: Oxford University Press, 1969), p. 64.
[3] Ibid., pp. 52-53.
[4] Ibid.
[5] Ibid.
[6] Samuel Eliot Morison, *The Oxford History of the American People* (New York: Oxford University Press, 1965), p. 64.
[7] Ibid., p. 65.
[8] John A. Garraty and Robert A. McCaughey, *The American Nation* (New York: Harper and Row, 1987), p. 22.
[9] Marshall and Manuel, pp. 161-162.

William Penn's Holy Experiment

[1] Morison, Commager and Leuchtenburg, p. 73.
[2] J.C. Furnas, *The Americans: a Social History of the United States, 1587-1914* (New York: G.P. Putnam's Sons, 1969), p. 80.
[3] Betty Ellen Haughey, *William Penn: American Pioneer* (New York: G.P. Putnam's Sons, 1968), p. 34.
[4] Morison, Commager and Leuchtenburg, p. 77.
[5] Hildegarde Dolson, *William Penn: Quaker Hero* (New York: Random House, 1961), p. 115.
[6] Ibid., p. 117.
[7] Morison, Commager and Leuchtenburg, p. '78.

The Great Awakening of a Friendship—and a Nation

[1] Morison, Commager and Leuchtenburg, pp. 107-108.
[2] Marshall and Manuel, p. 251.
[3] Carl Van Doren, *Benjamin Franklin* (New York: Viking Press, 1938), p. 131.
[4] Ibid., p. 135.
[5] Morison, Commager and Leuchtenburg, pp. 107-108.
[6] Marshall and Manuel, p. 249.
[7] Van Doren, p. 136.
[8] Ibid.
[9] Ibid.
[10] John Pollock, *George Whitefield and the Great Awakening* (New York: Doubleday, 1972), pp. 117-118.
[11] Van Doren, pp.136-137.
[12] Ibid., p. 137.
[13] Ibid.
[14] Ibid., pp. 137-138.
[15] Ibid., p. 138.

16 Rimas J. Orentas, "George Whitefield: Lightning Rod of the Great Awakening." Shippensburg UBF: A Symposium on Spiritual Leaders.

17 Pollock, pp. 121-122.

The American Revolution

1 John Bartlett, *Bartlett's Familiar Quotations* (Boston, MA: Little, Brown and Company, 1992), p. 339.

2 Marshall and Manuel, p. 306.

3 Ibid., pp. 307-308.

4 Ibid., p. 308.

5 Ibid., pp. 307-309.

6 Ibid., p. 309.

7 James Thomas Flexner, *Washington, the Indispensable Man* (New York: Signet, 1969), p. 80.

8 Marshall and Manuel, p. 312.

9 Ibid., p. 315.

10 Barbara Pollarine, *Great and Capital Changes: an Account of the Valley Forge Encampment* (Gettysburg, PA: Thomas Publications, 1993), p. 3.

11 Marshall and Manuel, p. 321.

12 Valley Forge National Historical Park pamphlet.

13 Flexner, p. 117.

14 Marshall and Manuel, p. 323.

15 Ibid., pp. 323-24.

16 Flexner, p. 118.

17 Esmond Wright, *Fabric of Freedom: 1763-1800* (New York: Hill and Wang, 1978), p. 135.

18 Marshall and Manuel, p. 326.

19 Rebecca Price Janney, *Great Women in American History* (Camp Hill, PA: Horizon Books, 1996), p. 175.

[20] Kathryn Cullen-DuPont, *The Encyclopedia of Women's History in America* (New York: Facts on File, 1996), p. 127.

[21] Janney, pp. 171-173; based on information obtained from Jan Gleiter and Kathleen Thompson, *Molly Pitcher* (Milwaukee: Raintree Publishers, 1987), pp. 4-22, 26-30.

John Marshall: Supreme Court Justice—and Every Man

[1] Peter Marshall and David Manuel, *From Sea to Shining Sea* (Grand Rapids, MI: Revell, 1986), pp. 203-4.

The Trail of Tears

[1] Marshall and Manuel, *From Sea to Shining Sea*, p. 351.

The Abolitionists

[1] Louis Ruchames, *The Abolitionists* (New York: Capricorn Books, 1963), p. 140.

[2] Ibid., p. 141.

[3] Ibid.

[4] Marshall and Manuel, *From Sea to Shining Sea*, p. 395.

[5] Ibid.

[6] Ibid. p. 402.

[7] Janney, pp. 231-233.

[8] Ibid., pp. 226-227.

[9] Ibid., pp. 221-222.

A Great Awakening for Theodore Weld

[1] Adapted from Marshall and Manuel, *From Sea to Shining Sea*, pp. 310-311.

The Civil War

[1] United States Christian Commission brochure, 1997.

[2] Alan Farley, ed. *The Christian Banner*, 13:2 (April/May/June/July 1997): Appomattox, VA, R.M.J.C., Inc., p. 8.

[3] Ibid., p. 9.

[4] General John B. Gordon, "Winter on the Rapidan—Religious Awakening." *The Christian Banner*, Vol. 13:2 (April/May/June/July 1997), Appomattox, VA, R.M.J.C., Inc.

[5] Ibid.

[6] Paul McClelland Angle, ed. *The Lincoln Reader* (New Brunswick, NJ: Rutgers University Press, 1947), pp. 508-510.

[7] "Gettysburg Address," Microsoft® Encarta® . Copyright 1994 Microsoft Corporation. Copyright 1994 Funk and Wagnall's Corporation.

[8] Stephen B. Oates, *With Malice Toward None* (New York: Harper and Row, 1977), p. 447.

[9] Angle, pp. 513-515.

The Frontier Life

[1] Janney, pp. 257-258.

Combating Demon Rum

[1] Furnas, p. 639.

[2] Pamphlet, "A Woman of Prayer" Evanston, IL: Signal Press, n.d.

The Great War

[1] "The History We Lived." U.S. New and World Report, 28 August/4 Sept. 1995, pp. 77-78.

[2] Theodore Roosevelt, *Foes of Our Own Household* (New York: Charles Scribner's Sons, 1917), p. 3.

[3] Gladys Williams, "Alvin Cullum York," http://voyager.rtd.utk.edu/volweb/Schools/York/biography.html (Courtesy of the Alvin C. York Agricultural Institute), p. 10.

[4] Ibid.

[5] This and all further statements by York are quoted from "Sgt. Alvin C. York's Diary," http://voyager.rtd.utk.edu/volweb/Schools/York/diary.html (Courtesy of the Alvin C. York Agricultural Institute).

[6] John Perry, *Sgt. York: His Life, Legend and Legacy* (Nashville: Broadman and Holman, 1997), p. 332.

Clarence Darrow's Dilemma

[1] Leon F. Litwack, et al. *The United States: Becoming a World Power* (Englewood Cliffs, NJ: Prentice-Hall, 1987), pp. 603-604.

[2] Joseph M. Stowell, *Following Christ* (Grand Rapids, MI: Zondervan, 1996), pp. 29-30.

World War II

[1] Richard Goff, et al. *The Twentieth Century* (New York: McGraw-Hill, 1994), p. 251.

[2] Alonzo L. Hamby, *The Imperial Years: The U.S. Since 1939* (New York: Longman, 1976), p. 39.

[3] Lewis Broad, *Winston Churchill: The Years of Achievement* (New York: Hawthorn Books, 1963), p. 136.

[4] Ibid., p. 137.

[5] Hamby, p. 43.

[6] Eric Larrabee, *Commander in Chief* (New York: Harper and Row, 1987), p. 240.

[7] Paul Fussell, "How the Leaders Led," *Newsweek, May 23, 1994,*pp. 36-38.

[8] Ibid.

[9] Wayne V. Hall, "A Pep Talk from Ike," *Stars and Stripes,* n.d.

[10] As recorded by Jim Garamone in "A Prayer for Overlord."

[11] Fussell, p. 37.

[12] Ibid.

[13] Ibid., p. 38.

Einsten's Humble Present

[1] "Einstein, Albert," *Compton's Reference Collection.* Copyright 1992, 1994, 1995 Compton's New Media, Inc. Copyright 1922-1995 Compton's Learning Company.

Harry Truman and the Founding of Modern Israel

[1] Merle Miller, *Plain Speaking: An Oral Biography of Harry S Truman* (New York: Berkeley Publishing, 1973), p. 213-218.

The Voice of the Century

[1] Janney, pp. 26-28.

A Decision for Life

[1] Author interview with Joe and Joyce Terry, August 17, 1994.

Man in Space

[1] "Space Exploration," Microsoft® Encarta® ; author interview with Dave Williams of the NASA Goddard Space Flight Center, Greenbelt, MD, July 18, 1997.

[2] "Apollo 13: To the Edge and Back," WGBM Educational Foundation, Boston, 1994.

The Asbury College Revival: God's Student Sit-in

[1] Robert E. Coleman, ed. *One Divine Moment* (Old Tappan, NY: Fleming H. Revell Company, 1970), pp. 83-84.

[2] Ibid., p. 84.

[3] Ibid., p. 85.

[4] Ibid., p. 89.

[5] Ibid., p. 90.

[6] Ibid., pp. 91-93.

There She Is, Miss America

[1] Heather Whitestone, "Listening with My Heart," *Crossings Corner*, Sept. 1997, p. 2.

[2] Ibid.

Bibliography

"Abolitionists," Microsoft® Encarta®. Copyright 1994 Microsoft Corporation. Copyright 1994 Funk and Wagnalls Corporation.

Ahlstrom, Sydney E. *A Religious History of the American People*. Garden City, NY: Image Books, 1975.

"Apollo 13: To the Edge and Back," WGBH Educational Foundation, Boston, 1994.

Athearn, Robert G. *American Heritage Illustrated History of the United States*. New York: Choice Publishing, 1988.

Athearn, Robert G. *American Heritage Illustrated History of the United States*, Volume 2: Colonial America. New York: Choice Publishing, 1988.

Athearn, Robert G. *American Heritage Illustrated History of the United States*, Volume 3: The Revolution. New York: Choice Publishing, 1988.

Bartlett, John. *Bartlett's Familiar Quotations*. Boston: Little, Brown and Company, 1992.

Brown, Dee. "The Trail of Tears." *American History*, Volume 1: Pre-colonial Through Reconstruction. Ed. Robert James Maddox. University Park, PA: Pennsylvania State University, 1989. pp. 129-135.

Churchill, Winston S. *Their Finest Hour*. New York: Bantam, 1962.

Coleman, Robert E., ed. *One Divine Moment*. Old Tappan, NJ: Fleming H. Revell Company, 1970.

Cullen-DuPont, Kathryn. *The Encyclopedia of Women's History in America*. New York: Facts on File, 1996.

Dolson, Hildegarde. *William Penn: Quaker Hero*. New York: Random House, 1961.

Divine, Robert A., et al. *America Past and Present*. New York: HarperCollins, 1995.

Dumoulin, Jim, "Apollo 13," November 28, 1996, NASA web page, ksc.nasa.gov/history/apollo/apollo-13.html.

Facial, Paul. "How the Leaders Led." *Newsweek* May 23 1994: 36-38.

Flexner, James Thomas. *Washington, the Indispensable Man*. New York: Signet, 1969.

Furnas, J.C. *The Americans: a Social History of the United States, 1587-1914*. New York: G.P. Putnam's Sons, 1969.

Garraty, John A., McCaughey, Robert A. *The American Nation*. New York: Harper and Row Publishers, 1987.

Gilbert, Martin. *The First World War: a Complete History*. New York: Henry Holt and Company, Inc., 1994.

Grant, George. *The Blood of the Moon*. Brentwood, TN: Wolgemuth & Hyatt, Publishers, Inc., 1991.

Gray, Daphne. *Yes, You Can, Heather!* Grand Rapids, MI: Zondervan, 1995.

Haughey, Betty Ellen. *William Penn: American Pioneer*. New York: G.P. Putnam's Sons, 1968.

Bibliography

"The History We Lived." *U.S. News and World Report,* 28 August/4 Sept. 1995: 77-78.

Janney, Rebecca Price. Interview with David Crawford, June 28, 1997.

Keegan, John. *The Second World War.* New York: Viking, 1989.

Litwack, Leon F., and Jordan, Winthrop D. *The United States: Becoming a World Power.* Englewood Cliffs, NJ: Prentice-Hall, 1987.

Marshall, Peter and Manuel, David. *The Light and the Glory.* Grand Rapids, MI: Fleming H. Revell, 1977.

Martin, James Kirby, Roberts, Randy, Mintz, Steven, McMurry, Linda O., Jones, James H., Haynes, Sam W. *A Concise History of America and its People.* New York: HarperCollins College Publishers, 1995.

Morison, Samuel Eliot. *The Oxford History of the American People.* New York: Oxford University Press, 1965.

Morison, Samuel Eliot, Commager, Henry Steele, and Leuchtenburg, William E. *The Growth of the American Republic,* Vol. 1. New York: Oxford University Press, 1969.

Orentas, Rimas J. "George Whitefield: Lightning Rod of the Great Awakening." Shippensburg UBF: A Symposium on Spiritual Leaders.

"Penn in the Capitol," "Penn and the Indians," "William Penn, Proprietor," http://xroads.virginia.edu/ cap/penn/pnintro.html.

"Penn, William," Microsoft® Encarta® . Copyright 1994 Microsoft Corporation. Copyright 1994 Funk & Wagnalls Corporation.

Pollarine, Barbara. *Great and Capital Changes: an Account of the Valley Forge Encampment*. Gettysburg, PA: Thomas Publications, 1993.

Pollock, John. *George Whitefield and the Great Awakening*. New York: Doubleday and Company, 1972.

Roosevelt, Theodore. *Foes of Our Own Household*. New York: Charles Scribner's Sons, 1917, p. 3.

Ruchames, Louis. *The Abolitionists*. New York: Capricorn Books, 1963, pp. 139-141. (All quotes, unless otherwise specified, are from this source.)

Strayer, Robert W. *The Making of the Modern World*. New York: St. Martin's Press, 1989.

Van Doran, Carl. *Benjamin Franklin*. New York: Viking Press, 1938.

Whitestone, Heather. "Listening With My Heart." *Crossings Corner* Sept. 1997: 2.

Wilson, R. Jackson, Gilbert, James, Nissenbaum, Stephen, Kupperman, Karen Ordahl, and Scott, Donald. *The Pursuit of Liberty*. Belmont, CA: Wadsworth Publishing Company, 1990.

Winthrop, John (1588-1649), Microsoft® Encarta® . Copyright 1994 Microsoft Corporation. Copyright 1994 Funk and Wagnalls Corporation.

Wright, Esmond. *Fabric of Freedom: 1763-1800*. New York: Hill and Wang, 1978.

Other Books by Rebecca Price Janney

Great Women in American History
(Adult non-fiction)

The Impossible Dreamers Series
(children's historic adventure series)

The Heather Reed Mystery Series
(children's mystery series)